ICE BOX
Crochet

LEISURE ARTS, INC.
Maumelle, Arkansas

EDITORIAL STAFF

Vice President of Editorial: Susan White Sullivan
Creative Art Director: Katherine Laughlin
Publications Director: Leah Lampirez
Special Projects Director: Susan Frantz Wiles
Technical Writer/Editor: Cathy Hardy
Technical Editors: Linda A. Daley, Sarah J. Green, and Lois J. Long
Art Category Manager: Lora Puls
Graphic Artist: Jacqueline Breazeal
Prepress Technician: Stephanie Johnson
Contributing Photographers: Jason Masters, Mark Mathews, and Ken West
Contributing Photo Stylist: Sondra Daniel and Lori Wenger

BUSINESS STAFF

President and Chief Executive Officer: Rick Barton
Senior Vice President of Operations: Jim Dittrich
Vice President of Finance: Fred F. Pruss
Vice President of Sales-Retail Books: Martha Adams
Vice President of Mass Market: Bob Bewighouse
Vice President of Technology and Planning: Laticia Mull Dittrich
Controller: Tiffany P. Childers
Information Technology Director: Brian Roden
Director of E-Commerce: Mark Hawkins
Manager of E-Commerce: Robert Young
Retail Customer Service Manager: Stan Raynor

Library of Congress Control Number: 2014934759

ISBN-13/EAN: 978-1-4647-0397-3
UPC: 0-28906-05836-9

Contents

ICE BOX CROCHET

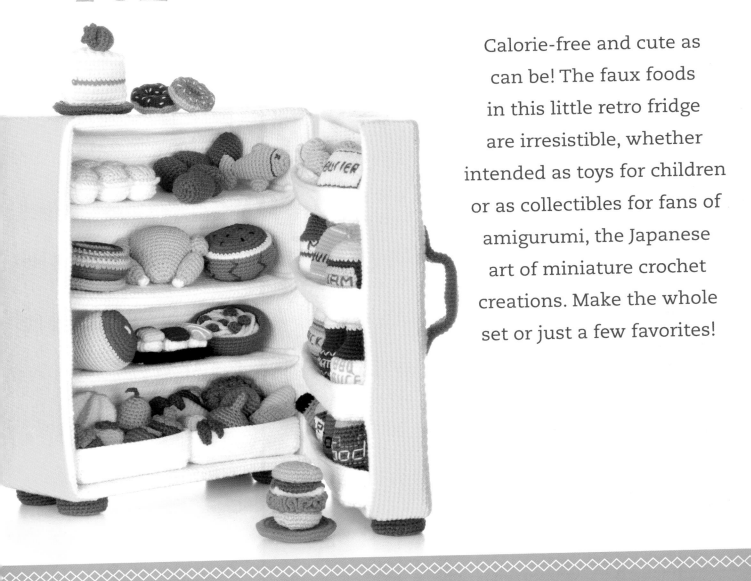

Calorie-free and cute as can be! The faux foods in this little retro fridge are irresistible, whether intended as toys for children or as collectibles for fans of amigurumi, the Japanese art of miniature crochet creations. Make the whole set or just a few favorites!

Meet the Designer

Wai Yee Ng

Since she learned to crochet at the age of 6, Wai Yee Ng has been fascinated by 3D designs. "I break away from conventional thinking and believe that nothing cannot be done," she says. "It's just the matter of how." The designer owns a craft shop near Kuala Lumpur in Malaysia and enjoys crochet, felt crafts, beading, and other hobbies.

ICE BOX

Yarn Weight

The photo model was made using fine weight yarns. You can also use light or medium weight yarns. The weight yarn you use will affect the gauge, as well as the hook size needed and the amount of yarn required.

Approximate Finished Size (assuming gauge is maintained)

Fine weight yarn: FINE 2

10" wide x 13" tall x 6½" deep (25.5 cm x 33 cm x 16.5 cm)

Light weight yarn: LIGHT 3

13" wide x 16½" tall x 8" deep (33 cm x 42 cm x 20.5 cm)

Medium weight yarn: MEDIUM 4

16" wide x 20" tall x 9½" deep (40.5 cm x 51 cm x 24 cm)

Yardage Needed

Use the table below as a guide when purchasing yarn for the Ice Box.

Color	#2 Fine FINE 2 yards (meters)	#3 Light LIGHT 3 yards (meters)	#4 Medium MEDIUM 4 yards (meters)
White	1,270 (1,161)	2,600 (2,377)	3,170 (2,899)
Yellow	650 (594)	1,300 (1,216)	1,625 (1,486)
Dk Brown	45 (41)	90 (82)	110 (101)

Crochet Hook Size & Gauge

A gauge is given for the Ice Box only *(see Gauge, page 94)*. Below is the approximate hook size and gauge for each weight of yarn.

Yarn Weight	Hook Size	Gauge 2" (5 cm) square
#2 Fine	B (2.25 mm)	13 sc & 14 rows/rnds
#3 Light	D (3.25 mm)	10 sc & 11 rows/rnds
#4 Medium	F (3.75 mm)	8 sc & 9 rows/rnds

FOOD ITEMS & DISHES

Yarn Weight and Finished Size

The photo models in this book were made using fine weight yarns. You can use light or medium weight yarns instead, but the resulting finished sizes will be larger. In order for your food to fit in the Ice Box as pictured on page 3, it's important that you use the same weight yarn for all of the food items as you do for the Ice Box.

If you are making the pieces for individual display, all of the pieces don't have to be made in the same weight yarn. For example, the turkey can be made in medium weight yarn and the carrots and potatoes in fine weight yarn, making the turkey a lot larger than the carrots and potatoes.

So that you can see the size difference, the examples below show the Bread and the Large Tray made in fine and medium weight yarns. The loaf of bread made in fine weight is 2" (4.5 cm) tall and the medium weight bread is 3" (7.5 cm) tall.

Yardage Needed

Exact yardages needed for the food items and the dishes are not given, as a skein of yarn will make many items. Most food items and dishes take less than 20 yards for fine weight, 45 yards for light weight, or 55 yards for medium weight.

Crochet Hook Size & Gauge

Below is the gauge for each weight of yarn and the recomended hook size.

Yarn Weight	Hook Size	Gauge 2" (5 cm) square
#2 Fine	B (2.25 mm)	14 sc & 14 rows/rnds
#3 Light	D (3.25 mm)	11 sc & 11 rows/rnds
#4 Medium	F (3.75 mm)	9 sc & 9 rows/rnds

Gauge is not critical when making the food or dishes. Use the size hook that will make your crochet fabric dense enough to prevent the stuffing from showing through your stitches.

Yarn Colors

The yarn colors needed are given with each individual project. We used 32 different colors, but you can use as many or as few shades of each color as desired.

For example, even though we used a total of 5 greens, most of the food items using a green can be made with any of the greens.

The colors used are as follows:

- ☐ Lime Green
- ☐ Lt Green
- ☐ Green
- ☐ Olive Green
- ☐ Dk Green
- ☐ White
- ☐ Grey
- ☐ Dk Grey
- ☐ Black
- ☐ Ecru
- ☐ Tan
- ☐ Lt Brown
- ☐ Brown
- ☐ Dk Brown
- ☐ Pink
- ☐ Lt Pink
- ☐ Dk Pink
- ☐ Rose
- ☐ Red
- ☐ Dk Red
- ☐ Orange
- ☐ Lt Yellow
- ☐ Yellow
- ☐ Chartreuse
- ☐ Dk Yellow
- ☐ Lt Blue
- ☐ Blue
- ☐ Dk Blue
- ☐ Navy
- ☐ Lt Purple
- ☐ Purple
- ☐ Dk Purple

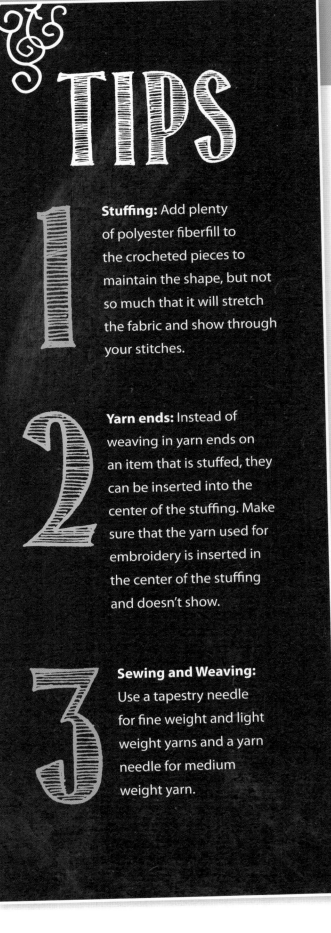

TIPS

1 **Stuffing:** Add plenty of polyester fiberfill to the crocheted pieces to maintain the shape, but not so much that it will stretch the fabric and show through your stitches.

2 **Yarn ends:** Instead of weaving in yarn ends on an item that is stuffed, they can be inserted into the center of the stuffing. Make sure that the yarn used for embroidery is inserted in the center of the stuffing and doesn't show.

3 **Sewing and Weaving:** Use a tapestry needle for fine weight and light weight yarns and a yarn needle for medium weight yarn.

·ICE BOX·

Our Ice Box was made using a fine weight yarn. You can also use light or medium weight yarn but the finished sizes will be larger than for a fine weight yarn. See Getting Started, page 4, for finished size, yarn, hook, and gauge information.

Finished Measurements: 10" wide x 13" tall x 6¹/₂" deep (25.5 cm x 33 cm x 16.5 cm)

 **EASY**

Shopping List

Yarn (Fine Weight)

☐ White - 1,270 yards (1,161 meters)

☐ Yellow - 650 yards (594 meters)

☐ Dk Brown - 45 yards (41 meters)

Crochet Hook

☐ Steel, size 2 (2.25 mm) **or** aluminum size B (2.25 mm) **or** size needed for gauge

Additional Supplies

☐ Tapestry needle

☐ Polyester fiberfill

☐ Cardboard or foam core board

☐ Adhesive tape (for bonding)

☐ Scissors

☐ Optional: Craft glue

GAUGE INFORMATION

13 sc and 14 rows/rnds = 2" (5 cm)

Gauge Swatch: 2" (5 cm) square

With Yellow, ch 14.

Row 1: Sc in second ch from hook and in each ch across: 13 sc.

Rows 2-14: Ch 1, turn; sc in each sc across.

Finish off.

——STITCH GUIDE——

SINGLE CROCHET 2 TOGETHER
(abbreviated sc2tog)

Pull up a loop in each of next 2 sc, YO and draw through all 3 loops on hook **(counts as one sc)**.

INSTRUCTIONS
Body
OUTER BODY
BACK

With Yellow, ch 65.

Row 1 (Wrong side): Sc in second ch from hook and in each ch across: 64 sc.

Note: Loop a short piece of yarn around the **back** of any stitch on Row 1 to mark **right** side and top edge.

Rows 2-88: Ch 1, turn; sc in each sc across; do **not** finish off.

SIDES

Rnd 1: Ch 1, do **not** turn; working around entire piece, skip first row, sc in end of next row and in each row across; sc in free loop of each ch across *(Fig. 2b, page 95)*; sc in end of each row across to last row, skip last row; sc in each sc across Row 88; join with slip st to first sc: 302 sc.

Rnds 2-32: Ch 1, sc in each sc around; join with slip st to first sc.

Finish off.

INNER BODY
BACK

With White, ch 63.

Row 1 (Wrong side): Sc in second ch from hook and in each ch across: 62 sc.

Note: Mark the **back** of any stitch on Row 1 as **right** side and top edge.

Rows 2-86: Ch 1, turn; sc in each sc across; do **not** finish off.

SIDES

Rnd 1: Ch 1, do **not** turn; working around entire piece, skip first row, sc in end of next row and in each row across; sc in free loop of each ch across; sc in end of each row across to last row, skip last row; sc in each sc across Row 86; join with slip st to first sc: 294 sc.

Rnds 2-32: Ch 1, sc in each sc around; join with slip st to first sc.

Finish off leaving a long end for sewing.

BODY ASSEMBLY

The measurements given below for the cardboard pieces are based on using fine weight yarn and achieving the gauge given for it. Adjustments will be needed if other yarn weights are used.

When instructed to cut a piece of cardboard, first measure the crocheted piece to be sure that the cardboard will be cut to the actual size, so it will fit nicely.

Cut a piece of cardboard 9$\frac{1}{2}$" x 12" (24 cm x 30.5 cm) and place it inside the Outer Body.

Cut a piece of cardboard 4$\frac{1}{4}$" x 44" (11 cm x 112 cm). Fold the cardboard 9$\frac{3}{4}$" (25 cm) from the edge, then 12$\frac{1}{4}$" (31 cm) from the first fold and 9$\frac{3}{4}$" (25 cm) from the second fold, leaving 12$\frac{1}{4}$" (31 cm) from the edge. Tape the two short edges together forming the last corner of an open cube. Place the cardboard inside the Outer Body against the Sides.

With **wrong** sides and top edges together, place the Inner Body on top of the cardboard. With White, whipstitch the pieces together *(Fig. 4a, page 96)*.

SHELF (Make 3)

With White, ch 61.

Row 1 (Wrong side): Sc in second ch from hook and in each ch across: 60 sc.

Note: Mark the **back** of any stitch on Row 1 as **right** side.

Rows 2-52: Ch 1, turn; sc in each sc across.

Finish off.

Cut a piece of cardboard 3¼" x 9" (8.5 cm x 23 cm).

EDGING

Row 1: Fold Shelf in half lengthwise with **wrong** side together. Working through **both** thicknesses and in end of rows, join White with sc in first row at fold (see Joining with Sc, page 95); sc in next row and in each row across; sc in each st across; insert cardboard, sc in end of each row across to fold: 112 sc.

Row 2: Ch 1, turn; sc in each sc across; finish off leaving a long end for sewing.

SHELF ASSEMBLY

Using photo as a guide for placement:

Insert a Shelf inside the Body, 2½" (6.5 cm) from the top, folding the Edging up to form a ridge along the Sides and Back of the Ice Box. With White, sew the Shelf in place, allowing ½" (1.2 cm) for the Door Tray to sit when the door is closed. Sew another Shelf 3" (7.5 cm) below the first Shelf.
Sew the remaining Shelf 3" (7.5 cm) below the previous Shelf.

Door
OUTER DOOR
FRONT & SIDES

Work same as Outer Body, page 8, through Rnd 11 of Sides: 302 sc.

Finish off.

INNER DOOR
FRONT & SIDES

Work same as Inner Body, page 8, through Rnd 11 of Sides: 294 sc.

Finish off leaving a long end for sewing.

DOOR ASSEMBLY

Cut a piece of cardboard 9½" x 12" (24 cm x 30.5 cm) and place it inside the Outer Door.

Cut a piece of cardboard 1¼" x 44" (3 cm x 112 cm). Fold the cardboard 9¾" (25 cm) from the edge, then 12¼" (31 cm) from the first fold and 9¾" (25 cm) from the second fold, leaving 12¼" (31 cm) from the edge. Tape the two short edges together forming the last corner of an open cube. Place the cardboard inside the Outer Door against the Sides.

With **wrong** sides and top edges together, place the Inner Door on top of the cardboard. With White, whipstitch the pieces together.

DOOR SHELF (Make 4)
BOTTOM

With White, ch 61.

Row 1 (Right side): Sc in second ch from hook and in each ch across: 60 sc.

Note: Mark Row 1 as **right** side.

Rows 2-15: Ch 1, turn; sc in each sc across.

Finish off.

TOP

Work same as Bottom; do **not** finish off.

Cut a piece of cardboard 2" x 9" (5 cm x 23 cm).

SIDES

Rnd 1: With **wrong** sides of Bottom and Top together, Top facing, and working through **both** thicknesses, ch 1, working around entire pieces, skip first row, sc in end of next row and in each row across; sc in free loops of each ch across; sc in end of each row across to last row, skip last row; insert cardboard, sc in each sc across; join with slip st to first sc: 148 sc.

Rnds 2-8: Ch 1, sc in each sc around; join with slip st to first sc.

Finish off.

SHELF ASSEMBLY

Note: The Shelves will stick out ¹/₂" (1.2 cm) from the edge of the Door.

Using photo as a guide for placement:
Sew a Shelf to the bottom of the Inner Door.
Sew the bottom of a Shelf in place 2¹/₂" (6.5 cm) from the top.
Sew the bottom of another Shelf 3" (7.5 cm) below the first Shelf.
Sew the bottom of the remaining Shelf 3" (7.5 cm) below the previous Shelf.

VEGETABLE TRAY (Make 2)
BOTTOM

With White, ch 29.

Row 1 (Wrong side)**:** Sc in second ch from hook and in each ch across: 28 sc.

Note: Mark the **back** of any stitch on Row 1 as **right** side.

Rows 2-24: Ch 1, turn; sc in each sc across.

Finish off.

TOP

Work same as Bottom; do **not** finish off.

Cut a piece of cardboard 3¹/₄" x 4" (8.5 cm x 10 cm).

SIDES

Rnd 1: With **wrong** sides of Bottom and Top together, Top facing, and working through **both** thicknesses, ch 1, working around entire pieces, skip first row, sc in end of next row and in each row across; sc in free loops of each ch across; sc in end of each row across to last row, skip last row; insert cardboard, sc in each sc across; join with slip st to first sc: 102 sc.

Rnds 2-8: Ch 1, sc in each sc around; join with slip st to first sc.

Finish off.

Hinge

With Yellow, ch 81.

Row 1: Sc in second ch from hook and in each ch across: 80 sc.

Rows 2-14: Ch 1, turn; sc in each sc across.

Finish off leaving a long end for sewing.

Note: The Hinge can be sewn on either side of the Body and Door to enable the Door to open in either direction.
Place the Body and Door together with the side you want the Hinge on facing up. Place the center length of the Hinge over the edge of the Body and the Door as shown below. Using the long end, whipstitch around the entire Hinge. With the Door open, whipstitch the center of the Hinge to the edge of the Door and also to the Body.

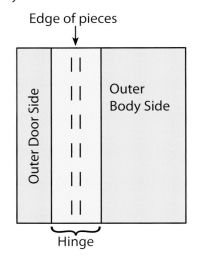

Edge of pieces

Outer Door Side | Outer Body Side

Hinge

Leg (Make 6)

With Dk Brown, ch 4; join with slip st to form a ring.

Rnd 1 (Right side)**:** Ch 1, 6 sc in ring; join with slip st to first sc.

Rnd 2: Ch 1, 2 sc in each sc around; join with slip st to first sc: 12 sc.

Rnd 3: Ch 1, 2 sc in same st as joining, sc in next sc, (2 sc in next sc, sc in next sc) around; join with slip st to first sc: 18 sc.

Rnd 4: Ch 1, 2 sc in same st as joining, sc in next 2 sc, (2 sc in next sc, sc in next 2 sc) around; join with slip st to first sc: 24 sc.

Rnd 5: Ch 1, 2 sc in same st as joining, sc in next 3 sc, (2 sc in next sc, sc in next 3 sc) around; join with slip st to first sc: 30 sc.

Rnd 6: Ch 1, sc in Back Loop Only of each sc around *(Fig. 1, page 95)*; join with slip st to **both** loops of first sc.

Rnds 7 and 8: Ch 1, sc in both loops of each sc around; join with slip st to first sc.

Finish off leaving a long end for sewing.

Stuff the Leg with polyester fiberfill.

Using photo as a guide for placement, sew 4 Legs to the Outer Body and 2 Legs to the Outer Door.

Handle

With Dk Brown and leaving a long end for sewing, ch 4; join with slip st to form a ring.

Rnd 1 (Right side)**:** Ch 1, 6 sc in ring; join with slip st to first sc.

Rnd 2: Ch 1, 2 sc in each sc around; join with slip st to first sc: 12 sc.

Rnd 3: Ch 1, 2 sc in same st as joining, sc in next 5 sc, 2 sc in next sc, sc in last 5 sc; join with slip st to first sc: 14 sc.

Rnd 4: Ch 1, 2 sc in same st as joining, sc in next 6 sc, 2 sc in next sc, sc in last 6 sc; join with slip st to first sc: 16 sc.

Rnd 5: Ch 1, 2 sc in same st as joining, sc in next 7 sc, 2 sc in next sc, sc in last 7 sc; join with slip st to first sc: 18 sc.

Rnds 6-32: Ch 1, sc in each sc around; join with slip st to first sc.

Rnd 33: Ch 1, beginning in same st as joining, (sc2tog, sc in next 7 sc) twice; join with slip st to first sc: 16 sc.

Rnd 34: Ch 1, beginning in same st as joining, (sc2tog, sc in next 6 sc) twice; join with slip st to first sc: 14 sc.

Rnd 35: Ch 1, beginning in same st as joining, (sc2tog, sc in next 5 sc) twice; join with slip st to first sc: 12 sc.

Rnd 36: Ch 1, beginning in same st as joining, sc2tog around; join with slip st to first sc, finish off leaving a long end for sewing: 6 sc.

Using photo as a guide for placement:
Sew the last 5 rnds of the Handle to the Door, 3½" (9 cm) from the top of the Ice Box and ½" (1.2 cm) from the outer edge (opposite edge as the Hinge).
Place Rnd 5 of the Handle approximately 2¾" (7 cm) from the sewn end and sew the first 5 rnds in place.

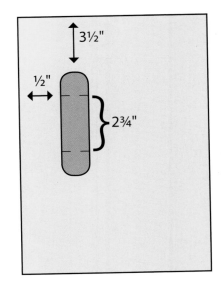

BREAD & CONDIMENTS

Every kitchen needs the basics: Bread, BBQ Sauce, Tomato Sauce, Pickles, Peanut Butter, and Jam.

 **EASY**

Shopping List

Yarn (Fine Weight)

Note: Light or Medium Weight yarn can be used, but the finished sizes will be slightly larger *(see Getting Started, page 4)*. See individual project for colors needed.

Crochet Hook

☐ Steel, size 2 (2.25 mm) **or** aluminum size B (2.25 mm) **or** size needed to achieve a dense gauge

Additional Supplies

☐ Tapestry needle
☐ Polyester fiberfill

GAUGE INFORMATION

Use the size hook needed to achieve a dense gauge *(see Crochet Hook Size & Gauge, page 5)*.

—————— STITCH GUIDE ——————

SINGLE CROCHET 2 TOGETHER *(abbreviated sc2tog)*
Pull up a loop in each of next 2 sc, YO and draw through all 3 loops on hook **(counts as one sc)**.

BREAD

Shown with Large Tray, page 89.

Finished Size: Approximately
   1³/₄" wide x 2" high (4.5 cm x 5 cm)
   Loaf: 2¹/₄" (5.5 cm) long

Yarn Colors
☐ Lt Brown
☐ White

SLICE
FIRST SIDE

With White, ch 11.

Row 1 (Wrong side)**:** Sc in second ch from hook and in each ch across: 10 sc.

Note: Loop a short piece of yarn around the **back** of any stitch on Row 1 to mark **right** side.

Rows 2-9: Ch 1, turn; sc in each sc across.

Row 10: Ch 1, turn; 2 sc in first sc, sc in next 8 sc, 2 sc in last sc: 12 sc.

Row 11: Ch 1, turn; 2 sc in first sc, sc in next 10 sc, 2 sc in last sc: 14 sc.

Row 12: Ch 1, turn; beginning in first sc, sc2tog, sc in next 10 sc, sc2tog; finish off: 12 sc.

Crust: With **right** side facing and working in end of rows, join Lt Brown with sc in Row 11 *(see Joining With Sc, page 95)*; working around entire piece, sc in next row and in each row across; sc in free loop of each ch across *(Fig. 2b, page 95)*; sc in end of each row across to last row, skip last row; sc in each sc across Row 12; join with slip st to first sc, finish off: 44 sc.

SECOND SIDE

Work same as First Side; finish off leaving a long end for sewing.

With **wrong** sides together and matching sts, whipstitch both pieces together *(Fig. 4a, page 96)*, stuffing the Slice lightly with polyester fiberfill before closing.

LOAF
FIRST END

Work same as First Side of Slice: 44 sc.

SECOND END

Work same as First Side of Slice; do **not** finish off at end of Crust (**counts as Rnd 1**): 44 sc.

CRUST

Rnds 2-13: Ch 1, sc in each sc around; join with slip st to first sc.

Finish off leaving a long end for sewing.

Stuff the Loaf with polyester fiberfill. Matching sts, whipstitch the First End to the Crust.

BBQ sauce

Finished Size: Approximately 1³/₄" wide x 2³/₄" high (4.5 cm x 7 cm)

Yarn Colors
- ☐ Dk Brown
- ☐ White
- ☐ Orange

BOTTLE
With Dk Brown, ch 9.

Rnd 1 (Right side)**:** Sc in second ch from hook and in next 6 chs, 3 sc in last ch; working in free loops of beginning ch *(Fig. 2b, page 95)*, sc in next 6 chs, 2 sc in next ch; join with slip st to first sc: 18 sc.

Rnd 2: Ch 1, 2 sc in same st as joining, sc in next 6 sc, 2 sc in each of next 3 sc, sc in next 6 sc, 2 sc in each of last 2 sc; join with slip st to first sc: 24 sc.

Rnd 3: Ch 1, 2 sc in same st as joining, sc in next 7 sc, 2 sc next sc, (sc in next sc, 2 sc in next sc) twice, sc in next 7 sc, (2 sc in next sc, sc in next sc) twice; join with slip st to first sc: 30 sc.

Rnd 4: Ch 1, sc in Back Loop Only of each sc around *(Fig. 1, page 95)*; join with slip st to **both** loops of first sc.

Rnds 5-11: Ch 1, sc in both loops of each sc around; join with slip st to first sc.

Rnd 12: Ch 1, beginning in same st as joining, sc2tog, sc in next 11 sc, sc2tog twice, sc in next 11 sc, sc2tog; join with slip st to first sc: 26 sc.

Stuff the Bottle with polyester fiberfill as you work.

Rnd 13: Ch 1, beginning in same st as joining, sc2tog, sc in next 9 sc, sc2tog twice, sc in next 9 sc, sc2tog; join with slip st to first sc: 22 sc.

Rnd 14: Ch 1, beginning in same st as joining, sc2tog, sc in next 7 sc, sc2tog twice, sc in next 7 sc, sc2tog; join with slip st to first sc: 18 sc.

Rnd 15: Ch 1, working in same st as joining, (sc2tog, sc in next sc) around; join with slip st to first sc: 12 sc.

Rnds 16 and 17: Ch 1, sc in each sc around; join with slip st to first sc.

Rnd 18: Ch 1, sc in each sc around; drop Dk Brown, with White, join with slip st to first sc *(Fig. 3c, page 96)*.

CAP
Rnds 1 and 2: Ch 1, sc in each sc around; join with slip st to first sc.

Rnd 3: Ch 1, working in Back Loops Only and beginning in same st as joining, sc2tog around; join with slip st to **both** loops of first sc, finish off leaving a long end for sewing: 6 sc.

Weave end through remaining sc *(Fig. 5, page 96)*; gather tightly to close and secure end.

LABEL
With White, ch 11.

Row 1: Sc in second ch from hook and in each ch across: 10 sc.

Rows 2-5: Ch 1, turn; sc in each sc across.

Finish off leaving a long end for sewing.

Using photo as a guide for placement:
With Orange, embroider "BBQ" on the Label across Rows 4 and 5 and "SAUCE" across Rows 1 and 2 using straight stitch *(Fig. 7, page 96)*.

Whipstitch the Label to the Bottle *(Figs. 4a & b, page 96)*.

TOMATO SAUCE

Finished Size: Approximately
1¹/₂" diameter x 2¹/₂" high
(4 cm x 6.5 cm)

Yarn Colors
- ☐ Dk Red
- ☐ Lt Pink
- ☐ Dk Yellow
- ☐ Lime Green

BOTTLE

With Dk Red, ch 4; join with slip st to form a ring.

Rnd 1 (Right side): Ch 1, 6 sc in ring; join with slip st to first sc.

Rnd 2: Ch 1, 2 sc in each sc around; join with slip st to first sc: 12 sc.

Rnd 3: Ch 1, 2 sc in same st as joining, sc in next sc, (2 sc in next sc, sc in next sc) around; join with slip st to first sc: 18 sc.

Rnd 4: Ch 1, sc in same st as joining and in next sc, 2 sc in next sc, (sc in next 2 sc, 2 sc in next sc) around; join with slip st to first sc: 24 sc.

Rnd 5: Ch 1, sc in same st as joining, 2 sc in next sc, (sc in next 3 sc, 2 sc in next sc) around to last 2 sc, sc in last 2 sc; join with slip st to first sc: 30 sc.

Rnds 6-13: Ch 1, sc in each sc around; join with slip st to first sc.

Rnd 14: Ch 1, sc in same st as joining and in next 2 sc, sc2tog, (sc in next 3 sc, sc2tog) around; join with slip st to first sc: 24 sc.

Rnd 15: Ch 1, beginning in same st as joining, (sc2tog, sc in next 2 sc) around; join with slip st to first sc: 18 sc.

Rnds 16-18: Ch 1, sc in each sc around; join with slip st to first sc.

Stuff the Bottle with polyester fiberfill as you work.

Rnd 19: Ch 1, sc in each sc around; cut Dk Red, with Lt Pink, join with slip st to first sc (*Fig. 3c, page 96*).

CAP

Rnds 1 and 2: Ch 1, sc in each sc around; join with slip st to first sc.

Rnd 3: Ch 1, working in Back Loops Only (*Fig. 1, page 95*), sc in same st as joining, sc2tog, (sc in next sc, sc2tog) around; join with slip st to **both** loops of first sc: 12 sc.

Rnd 4: Ch 1, working in both loops and beginning in same st as joining, sc2tog around; join with slip st to first sc, finish off leaving a long end for sewing: 6 sc.

Weave end through remaining sc (*Fig. 5, page 96*); gather tightly to close and secure end.

Using photo as a guide for placement:
With Dk Yellow, embroider "TOMATO" on the Bottle across Rnds 10 and 11 using straight stitch (*Fig. 7, page 96*).

Using Lime Green, embroider a zigzag stitch around Rnd 8 and around Rnd 13 of Bottle.

PICKLES

Finished Size: Approximately
1³/₄" diameter x 2¹/₂" high
(4.5 cm x 6.5 cm)

Yarn Colors
- ☐ Lt Green
- ☐ Lt Yellow
- ☐ Dk Yellow
- ☐ Brown

JAR
With Lt Green, ch 4; join with slip st to form a ring.

Rnd 1 (Right side)**:** Ch 1, 6 sc in ring; join with slip st to first sc.

Note: Loop a short piece of yarn around any stitch to mark Rnd 1 as **right** side.

Rnd 2: Ch 1, 2 sc in each sc around; join with slip st to first sc: 12 sc.

Rnd 3: Ch 1, 2 sc in same st as joining, sc in next sc, (2 sc in next sc, sc in next sc) around; join with slip st to first sc: 18 sc.

Rnd 4: Ch 1, sc in same st as joining and in next sc, 2 sc in next sc, (sc in next 2 sc, 2 sc in next sc) around; join with slip st to first sc: 24 sc.

Rnd 5: Ch 1, sc in same st as joining, 2 sc in next sc, (sc in next 3 sc, 2 sc in next sc) around to last 2 sc, sc in last 2 sc; join with slip st to first sc: 30 sc.

Rnd 6: Ch 1, sc in same st as joining and in next 3 sc, 2 sc in next sc, (sc in next 4 sc, 2 sc in next sc) around; join with slip st to first sc: 36 sc.

Rnd 7: Ch 1, working in Back Loops Only *(Fig. 1, page 95)*, sc in each sc around; join with slip st to **both** loops of first sc.

Rnds 8-16: Ch 1, sc in both loops of each sc around; join with slip st to first sc.

Rnd 17: Ch 1, sc in each sc around; cut Lt Green, with Lt Yellow, join with slip st to first sc *(Fig. 3c, page 96)*.

Rnds 18 and 19: Ch 1, sc in each sc around; join with slip st to first sc.

Finish off.

LID
With Lt Yellow, work same as Jar through Rnd 6: 36 sc.

Finish off leaving a long end for sewing.

LABEL
With Dk Yellow, ch 15.

Row 1: Sc in second ch from hook and in each ch across: 14 sc.

Rows 2-4: Ch 1, turn; sc in each sc across.

Finish off leaving a long end for sewing.

Using photo as a guide for placement:
With Brown, embroider "PICKLES!" on the Label across Rows 2 and 3 using straight stitch *(Fig. 7, page 96)*.

Whipstitch the Label to the Jar *(Figs. 4a & b, page 96)*.

With Brown, embroider a line on the Jar that goes around the Label using backstitch *(Fig. 6, page 96)*.

Whipstitch the Lid to the Jar, stuffing the Jar with polyester fiberfill before closing.

PEANUT BUTTER

Finished Size: Approximately 2" diameter x 2¼" high (5 cm x 5.5 cm)

Yarn Colors
- ☐ Lt Brown
- ☐ Dk Brown
- ☐ Dk Yellow

JAR

With Lt Brown, ch 4; join with slip st to form a ring.

Rnd 1 (Right side)**:** Ch 1, 6 sc in ring; join with slip st to first sc.

Note: Loop a short piece of yarn around any stitch to mark Rnd 1 as **right** side.

Rnd 2: Ch 1, 2 sc in each sc around; join with slip st to first sc: 12 sc.

Rnd 3: Ch 1, 2 sc in same st as joining, sc in next sc, (2 sc in next sc, sc in next sc) around; join with slip st to first sc: 18 sc.

Rnd 4: Ch 1, sc in same st as joining and in next sc, 2 sc in next sc, (sc in next 2 sc, 2 sc in next sc) around; join with slip st to first sc: 24 sc.

Rnd 5: Ch 1, sc in same st as joining, 2 sc in next sc, (sc in next 3 sc, 2 sc in next sc) around to last 2 sc, sc in last 2 sc; join with slip st to first sc: 30 sc.

Rnd 6: Ch 1, sc in same st as joining and in next 3 sc, 2 sc in next sc, (sc in next 4 sc, 2 sc in next sc) around; join with slip st to first sc: 36 sc.

Rnd 7: Ch 1, 2 sc in same st as joining, sc in next 5 sc, (2 sc in next sc, sc in next 5 sc) around; join with slip st to first sc: 42 sc.

Rnds 8-14: Ch 1, sc in each sc around; join with slip st to first sc.

Rnd 15: Ch 1, sc in same st as joining and in next 4 sc, sc2tog, (sc in next 5 sc, sc2tog) around; cut Lt Brown, with Dk Yellow, join with slip st to first sc *(Fig. 3c, page 96)*: 36 sc.

Rnds 16 and 17: Ch 1, sc in each sc around; join with slip st to first sc.

Finish off.

LID

With Dk Yellow, work same as Jar through Rnd 6: 36 sc.

Finish off leaving a long end for sewing.

LABEL

With Dk Brown, ch 15.

Row 1: Sc in second ch from hook and in each ch across: 14 sc.

Rows 2-7: Ch 1, turn; sc in each sc across.

Finish off leaving a long end for sewing.

Using photo as a guide for placement:
With Dk Yellow, embroider "Peanut" on the Label across Rows 5 and 6 and "butter" across Rows 2 and 3 using straight stitch *(Fig. 7, page 96)*.

Whipstitch the Label to the Jar *(Figs. 4a & b, page 96)*.

Whipstitch the Lid to the Jar, stuffing the Jar with polyester fiberfill before closing.

Finished Size: Approximately
2" diameter x 2$\frac{1}{4}$" high
(5 cm x 5.5 cm)

Yarn Colors

- ☐ Dk Red
- ☐ Pink
- ☐ Lt Purple
- ☐ Dk Purple

JAR

With Dk Red, ch 4; join with slip st to form a ring.

Rnd 1 (Right side)**:** Ch 1, 6 sc in ring; join with slip st to first sc.

Note: Loop a short piece of yarn around any stitch to mark Rnd 1 as **right** side.

Rnd 2: Ch 1, 2 sc in each sc around; join with slip st to first sc: 12 sc.

Rnd 3: Ch 1, 2 sc in same st as joining, sc in next sc, (2 sc in next sc, sc in next sc) around; join with slip st to first sc: 18 sc.

Rnd 4: Ch 1, sc in same st as joining and in next sc, 2 sc in next sc, (sc in next 2 sc, 2 sc in next sc) around; join with slip st to first sc: 24 sc.

Rnd 5: Ch 1, sc in same st as joining, 2 sc in next sc, (sc in next 3 sc, 2 sc in next sc) around to last 2 sc, sc in last 2 sc; join with slip st to first sc: 30 sc.

Rnd 6: Ch 1, sc in same st as joining and in next 3 sc, 2 sc in next sc, (sc in next 4 sc, 2 sc in next sc) around; join with slip st to first sc: 36 sc.

Rnd 7: Ch 1, 2 sc in same st as joining, sc in next 5 sc, (2 sc in next sc, sc in next 5 sc) around; join with slip st to first sc: 42 sc.

Rnds 8-14: Ch 1, sc in each sc around; join with slip st to first sc.

Rnd 15: Ch 1, sc in same st as joining and in next 4 sc, sc2tog, (sc in next 5 sc, sc2tog) around; cut Dk Red, with Pink, join with slip st to first sc *(Fig. 3c, page 96)*: 36 sc.

Rnds 16 and 17: Ch 1, sc in each sc around; join with slip st to first sc.

Finish off.

LID

With Pink, work same as Jar through Rnd 6: 36 sc.

Finish off leaving a long end for sewing.

LABEL

With Lt Purple, ch 9.

Row 1: Sc in second ch from hook and in each ch across: 8 sc.

Rows 2-4: Ch 1, turn; sc in each sc across.

Finish off leaving a long end for sewing.

Using photo as a guide for placement:
With Dk Purple, embroider "JAM" on the Label across Rows 2 and 3 using straight stitch *(Fig. 7, page 96)*.

Whipstitch the Label to the Jar *(Figs. 4a & b, page 96)*.

Whipstitch the Lid to the Jar, stuffing the Jar with polyester fiberfill before closing.

DAIRY

Stock up on fresh Milk, Cheese, Butter, and a Carton of Eggs.

 **EASY**

Shopping List

Yarn (Fine Weight)

Note: Light or Medium Weight yarn can be used, but the finished sizes will be slightly larger *(see Getting Started, page 4)*. See individual project for colors needed.

Crochet Hook

☐ Steel, size 2 (2.25 mm) **or** aluminum size B (2.25 mm)
  or size needed to achieve a dense gauge

Additional Supplies

☐ Tapestry needle
☐ Polyester fiberfill
☐ Optional: card stock (for Milk)

GAUGE INFORMATION

Use the size hook needed to achieve a dense gauge *(see Crochet Hook Size & Gauge, page 5)*.

─── STITCH GUIDE ───

SINGLE CROCHET 2 TOGETHER *(abbreviated sc2tog)*

Pull up a loop in each of next 2 sc, YO and draw through all 3 loops on hook **(counts as one sc)**.

Finished Size: Approximately 1¾" wide x 2¼" high (4.5 cm x 5.5 cm)

Yarn Colors

- ☐ White
- ☐ Dk Blue
- ☐ Blue
- ☐ Red

BOTTOM

With White, ch 11.

Row 1 (Right side): Sc in second ch from hook and in each ch across: 10 sc.

Note: Loop a short piece of yarn around any stitch to mark Row 1 as **right** side.

Rows 2-11: Ch 1, turn; sc in each sc across.

SIDES

Rnd 1: Ch 1, do **not** turn; working around entire piece, skip first row, sc in end of next row and in each row across; sc in free loop of each ch across *(Fig. 2b, page 95)*; working in end of rows, sc in each row across to last row, skip last row; sc in each sc across Row 11; join with slip st to first sc: 40 sc.

Rnds 2-4: Ch 1, sc in each sc around; join with slip st to first sc.

Rnd 5: Ch 1, sc in each sc around; drop White, with Dk Blue, join with slip st to first sc *(Fig. 3c, page 96)*.

Rnd 6: Ch 1, sc in each sc around; drop Dk Blue, with White, join with slip st to first sc.

Rnds 7 and 8: Ch 1, sc in each sc around; join with slip st to first sc.

Rnd 9: Ch 1, sc in each sc around; cut White, with Dk Blue, join with slip st to first sc.

Rnd 10: Ch 1, sc in each sc around; join with slip st to first sc.

Rnd 11: Ch 1, sc in Back Loop Only of each sc around *(Fig. 1, page 95)*; join with slip st to **both** loops of first sc.

Rnds 12-15: Ch 1, sc in both loops of each sc around; join with slip st to first sc.

Rnd 16: Ch 1, sc in same st as joining and in each sc around to last 8 sc, place marker in sc just made for Tab placement, sc in last 8 sc; join with slip st to first sc, do **not** finish off.

Note: A strip of card stock, cut to the dimensions of the Sides, can be inserted in the piece for stability.

Stuff the Carton with polyester fiberfill to second Dk Blue rnd.

TAB

Row 1: Ch 1, fold top edge in half, working through **both** thicknesses, and beginning in same st as joining and in marked sc, sc in first 12 sc, leave remaining 8 sc unworked: 12 sc.

Row 2: Ch 1, turn; sc in each sc across; finish off.

Fold unworked sc on each side of Tab inward and tack in place.

CAP

With Blue, ch 4; join with slip st to form a ring.

Rnd 1 (Right side): Ch 1, 6 sc in ring; join with slip st to first sc.

Rnd 2: Ch 1, sc in Back Loop Only of each sc around; join with slip st to **both** loops of first sc, finish off leaving a long end for sewing.

Sew the Cap to the top of the Milk Carton.

Using photo as a guide for placement: With Red, embroider "MILK" on Rnds 8 and 9 of Sides using straight stitch *(Fig. 7, page 96)*.

Finished Size: Approximately 3"
diameter x 1¼" high
(7.5 cm x 3 cm)

Yarn Colors
- ☐ Tan
- ☐ Dk Yellow

BOTTOM

With Tan, ch 4; join with slip st to form a ring.

Row 1 (Right side)**:** Ch 1, 5 sc in ring; do **not** join.

Note: Loop a short piece of yarn around any stitch to mark Row 1 as **right** side.

Row 2: Ch 1, turn; 2 sc in each sc across: 10 sc.

Row 3: Ch 1, turn; 2 sc in first sc, sc in next sc, (2 sc in next sc, sc in next sc) across: 15 sc.

Row 4: Ch 1, turn; 2 sc in first sc, sc in next 2 sc, (2 sc in next sc, sc in next 2 sc) across: 20 sc.

Row 5: Ch 1, turn; 2 sc in first sc, sc in next 3 sc, (2 sc in next sc, sc in next 3 sc) across: 25 sc.

Row 6: Ch 1, turn; 2 sc in first sc, sc in next 4 sc, (2 sc in next sc, sc in next 4 sc) across: 30 sc.

Row 7: Ch 1, turn; 2 sc in first sc, sc in next 5 sc, (2 sc in next sc, sc in next 5 sc) across: 35 sc.

Row 8: Ch 1, turn; 2 sc in first sc, sc in next 6 sc, (2 sc in next sc, sc in next 6 sc) across: 40 sc.

Row 9: Ch 1, turn; 2 sc in first sc, sc in next 7 sc, (2 sc in next sc, sc in next 7 sc) across; finish off leaving a long end for sewing: 45 sc.

TOP

Work same as Bottom through Rnd 8: 40 sc.

Row 9: Ch 1, turn; 2 sc in first sc, (sc in next 7 sc, 2 sc in next sc) across to last 7 sc, sc in next 6 sc, sc in last sc changing to Dk Yellow *(Fig. 3a, page 96)*, cut Tan: 45 sc.

SIDES

Rnd 1: Ch 1, do **not** turn; working around entire piece, skip first row, sc in end of next 8 rows, sc in ring, sc in next 8 rows changing to Tan in last sc made *(Fig. 3b, page 96)*, cut Dk Yellow, skip last row; sc in Back Loop Only of each sc across Row 9 *(Fig. 1, page 95)*; cut Tan, with Dk Yellow, join with slip st to **both** loops of first sc: 62 sc.

Rnds 2-5: Ch 1, working in both loops, sc in same st as joining and in next 16 sc changing to Tan in last sc made, cut Dk Yellow, sc in each sc across; cut Tan, with Dk Yellow, join with slip st to first sc.

Rnd 6: Ch 1, sc in same st as joining and in next 16 sc changing to Tan in last sc made, cut Dk Yellow, sc in each sc across; join with slip st to first sc, finish off.

With **wrong** sides together and matching sts, whipstitch the Bottom to the Sides *(Figs. 4a & b, page 96)*, stuffing the Cheese with polyester fiberfill before closing.

BUTTER

Finished Size: Approximately 1³/₄" wide x 2³/₄" long (4.5 cm x 7 cm)

Yarn Colors
- ☐ Yellow
- ☐ Lt Yellow
- ☐ Olive Green
- ☐ Brown

BOTTOM

With Yellow, ch 11.

Row 1 (Wrong side)**:** Sc in second ch from hook and in each ch across: 10 sc.

Note: Loop a short piece of yarn around the **back** of any stitch on Row 1 to mark **right** side.

Rows 2-16: Ch 1, turn; sc in each sc across.

SIDES

Rnd 1: Ch 1, do **not** turn; working around entire piece, skip first row, sc in end of next row and in each row across; sc in free loop of each ch across *(Fig. 2b, page 95)*; sc in end of each row across to last row, skip last row; sc in each sc across Row 16; join with slip st to first sc: 50 sc.

Rnds 2-5: Ch 1, sc in each sc around; join with slip st to first sc.

Finish off.

TOP

With Lt Yellow, ch 12.

Row 1 (Right side)**:** Sc in second ch from hook and in each ch across: 11 sc.

Note: Mark Row 1 as **right** side.

Rows 2-17: Ch 1, turn; sc in each sc across.

SIDES

Rnd 1: Ch 1, do **not** turn; working around entire piece, skip first row, sc in end of next row and in each row across; sc in free loop of each ch across; sc in end of each row across to last row, skip last row; sc in each sc across Row 17; join with slip st to first sc: 54 sc.

Rnd 2: Ch 1, sc in each sc around; join with slip st to first sc, finish off.

Using photo as a guide for placement:
With Olive Green, embroider "BUTTER" on the Cover using straight stitch *(Fig. 7, page 96)*.
With Brown, embroider lines for decoration using backstitch *(Fig. 6, page 96)*.

Stuff the Bottom with polyester fiberfill.

Place the last 2 rnds of the Top over the last 2 rnds of the Bottom, and whipstitch the Top in place *(Fig. 4a, page 96)*.

CARTON OF EGGS

Finished Size: Approximately 2¹/₂" wide x 3³/₄" long (6.5 cm x 9.5 cm)

Yarn Colors
- ☐ Lt Yellow
- ☐ Ecru

CARTON

SECTION (Make 6)

With Lt Yellow, ch 5; join with slip st to form a ring.

Rnd 1 (Wrong side): Ch 1, 8 sc in ring; join with slip st to first sc.

Note: Loop a short piece of yarn around the **back** of any stitch on Rnd 1 to mark **right** side.

Rnd 2: Ch 1, 2 sc in same st as joining, sc in next sc, (2 sc in next sc, sc in next sc) around; join with slip st to first sc: 12 sc.

Rnd 3: Ch 1, 2 sc in same st as joining, sc in next 2 sc, (2 sc in next sc, sc in next 2 sc) around; join with slip st to first sc: 16 sc.

Rnd 4: Ch 1, 2 sc in same st as joining, sc in next 3 sc, (2 sc in next sc, sc in next 3 sc) around; join with slip st to first sc: 20 sc.

Rnd 5: Ch 1, sc in each sc around; join with slip st to first sc.

Rnd 6: Ch 1, working in Back Loops Only *(Fig. 1, page 95)*, 3 sc in same st as joining (corner), sc in next 4 sc, (3 sc in next sc, sc in next 4 sc) around; join with slip st to **both** loops of first sc, finish off: 28 sc.

With **wrong** sides together, whipstitch Rnd 6 of the Sections together *(Fig. 4a, page 96)*, arranging them in 2 rows of 3, working across 6 sc on each side and leaving center sc of each corner 3-sc group unworked.

EGGS (Make 6)

With Ecru, ch 4; join with slip st to form a ring.

Rnd 1 (Right side): Ch 1, 6 sc in ring; join with slip st to first sc.

Rnd 2: Ch 1, 2 sc in each sc around; join with slip st to first sc: 12 sc.

Rnd 3: Ch 1, 2 sc in same st as joining, sc in next sc, (2 sc in next sc, sc in next sc) around; join with slip st to first sc: 18 sc.

Rnds 4 and 5: Ch 1, sc in each sc around; join with slip st to first sc.

Stuff the Egg with polyester fiberfill as you work.

Rnd 6: Ch 1, sc in same st as joining, sc2tog, (sc in next sc, sc2tog) around; join with slip st to first sc: 12 sc.

Rnds 7 and 8: Ch 1, sc in each sc around; join with slip st to first sc.

Rnd 9: Ch 1, beginning in same st as joining, sc2tog around; join with slip st to first sc, finish off leaving a long end for sewing: 6 sc.

Weave end through remaining sc *(Fig. 5, page 96)*; gather tightly to close and secure end.

· DRINKS ·

For refreshments throughout the day, reach for a Cup of Coffee, Water Bottle,
Ice Tray, Soda & Cola, Beer, or Orange Juice.

◀■■□□▷ **EASY**

Shopping List

Yarn (Fine Weight)

Note: Light or Medium Weight yarn can be used, but the
finished sizes will be slightly larger *(see Getting Started,
page 4)*. See individual project for colors needed.

Crochet Hook
☐ Steel, size 2 (2.25 mm) **or** aluminum size B (2.25 mm)

   or size needed to achieve a dense gauge

Additional Supplies
☐ Tapestry needle
☐ Polyester fiberfill

GAUGE INFORMATION
Use the size hook needed to achieve a dense gauge *(see
Crochet Hook Size & Gauge, page 5)*.

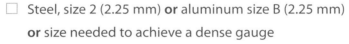

─── STITCH GUIDE ───
SINGLE CROCHET 2 TOGETHER *(abbreviated sc2tog)*
Pull up a loop in each of next 2 sc, YO and draw through all
3 loops on hook **(counts as one sc)**.

CUP OF COFFEE

Finished Size: Approximately 1³/₄" diameter x 2" high (4.5 cm x 5 cm)

Yarn Colors
- ☐ Lime Green
- ☐ Brown

CUP

With Lime Green, ch 4; join with slip st to form a ring.

Rnd 1 (Right side): Ch 1, 6 sc in ring; join with slip st to first sc.

Note: Loop a short piece of yarn around any stitch to mark Rnd 1 as **right** side.

Rnd 2: Ch 1, 2 sc in each sc around; join with slip st to first sc: 12 sc.

Rnd 3: Ch 1, 2 sc in same st as joining, sc in next sc, (2 sc in next sc, sc in next sc) around; join with slip st to first sc: 18 sc.

Rnd 4: Ch 1, 2 sc in same st as joining, sc in next 2 sc, (2 sc in next sc, sc in next 2 sc) around; join with slip st to first sc: 24 sc.

Rnd 5: Ch 1, 2 sc in same st as joining, sc in next 3 sc, (2 sc in next sc, sc in next 3 sc) around; join with slip st to first sc: 30 sc.

Rnd 6: Ch 1, 2 sc in same st as joining, sc in next 4 sc, (2 sc in next sc, sc in next 4 sc) around; join with slip st to first sc: 36 sc.

Rnd 7: Ch 1, sc in Back Loop Only of each sc around *(Fig. 1, page 95)*; join with slip st to **both** loops of first sc.

Rnds 8-19: Ch 1, sc in both loops of each sc around; join with slip st to first sc.

Finish off.

COFFEE

With Brown, work same as Cup through Rnd 6: 36 sc.

Finish off leaving a long end for sewing.

Stuff the Cup with polyester fiberfill.

Whipstitch the top of Rnd 6 of the Coffee to Rnd 17 of the Cup *(Fig. 4a, page 96)*, leaving 2 rnds above the Coffee.

HANDLE

With Lime Green and leaving a long end for sewing, ch 6; join with slip st to form a ring.

Rnd 1 (Right side): Ch 1, sc in each ch around; join with slip st to first sc: 6 sc.

Rnds 2-10: Ch 1, sc in each sc around; join with slip st to first sc.

Finish off leaving a long end for sewing.

Using photo as a guide for placement, sew the Handle to the side of the Cup placing one end on Rnds 9 and 10, and the other end on Rnds 15 and 16.

WATER BOTTLE

Finished Size: Approximately 1¼" diameter x 2½" high (3 cm x 6.5 cm)

Yarn Colors
- ☐ Blue
- ☐ Navy
- ☐ Dk Purple

BOTTLE

With Blue, ch 4; join with slip st to form a ring.

Rnd 1 (Right side): Ch 1, 6 sc in ring; join with slip st to first sc.

Rnd 2: Ch 1, 2 sc in each sc around; join with slip st to first sc: 12 sc.

Rnd 3: Ch 1, 2 sc in same st as joining, sc in next sc, (2 sc in next sc, sc in next sc) around; join with slip st to first sc: 18 sc.

Rnd 4: Ch 1, sc in same st as joining and in next sc, 2 sc in next sc, (sc in next 2 sc, 2 sc in next sc) around; join with slip st to first sc: 24 sc.

Rnd 5: Ch 1, sc in Back Loop Only of each sc around *(Fig. 1, page 95)*; join with slip st to **both** loops of first sc.

Rnds 6-12: Ch 1, sc in both loops of each sc around; join with slip st to first sc.

Stuff the Water Bottle with polyester fiberfill as you work.

Rnd 13: Ch 1, beginning in same st as joining, (sc2tog, sc in next 2 sc) around; join with slip st to first sc: 18 sc.

Rnds 14 and 15: Ch 1, sc in each sc around; join with slip st to first sc.

Rnd 16: Ch 1, sc in same st as joining, sc2tog, (sc in next sc, sc2tog) around; join with slip st to first sc: 12 sc.

Rnd 17: Ch 1, sc in each sc around; cut Blue, with Navy, join with slip st to first sc *(Fig. 3c, page 96)*.

Rnds 18 and 19: Ch 1, sc in each sc around; join with slip st to first sc.

Rnd 20: Ch 1, working in Back Loops Only and beginning in same st as joining, sc2tog around; join with slip st to **both** loops of first sc, finish off leaving a long end for sewing: 6 sc.

Weave end through remaining sc *(Fig. 5, page 96)*; gather tightly to close and secure end.

Using photo as a guide for placement:
With Dk Purple, embroider "H20" across Rnds 10 and 11 using straight stitch *(Fig. 7, page 96)*.

ICE TRAY

Finished Size: Approximately 2¹/₄" wide x 4" long (5.5 cm x 10 cm)

Yarn Colors
- ☐ White
- ☐ Lt Blue

TRAY SECTION (Make 6)

BOTTOM
With White, ch 7.

Row 1: Sc in second ch from hook and in each ch across: 6 sc.

Rows 2-6: Ch 1, turn; sc in each sc across.

SIDES
Rnd 1 (Right side): Ch 1, do **not** turn; working around entire piece, skip first row, sc in end of last 5 rows; sc in free loop of each ch across (*Fig. 2b, page 95*); sc in end of each row across to last row, skip last row; sc in each sc across Row 6; join with slip st to first sc: 22 sc.

Note: Loop a short piece of yarn around any stitch to mark Rnd 1 as **right** side.

Rnds 2-4: Ch 1, sc in each sc around; join with slip st to first sc.

Rnd 5: Ch 1, working in Front Loops Only (*Fig. 1, page 95*), 3 sc in same st as joining (corner), sc in next 4 sc, 3 sc in next sc, sc in next 5 sc, 3 sc in next sc, sc in next 4 sc, 3 sc in next sc, sc in last 5 sc; join with slip st to **both** loops of first sc, finish off leaving a long end for sewing: 30 sc.

Placing the Bottom of all Tray Sections in the same direction and with **wrong** sides together, whipstitch Rnd 5 of the Sides together (*Fig. 4a, page 96*), arranging them in 2 rows of 3 and leaving center sc of each corner 3-sc group unworked.

ICE CUBE (Make 6)
With Lt Blue, work same as Tray Section through Rnd 1 of Sides: 22 sc.

Finish off leaving a long end for sewing.

Whipstitch top of Rnd 1 of each Ice Cube to free loops (*Fig. 2a, page 95*) of Rnd 4 on each Tray Section, stuffing each Section with polyester fiberfill before closing.

SODA & COLA

BOTTOM

With Grey, ch 4; join with slip st to form a ring.

Rnd 1 (Right side): Ch 1, 6 sc in ring; join with slip st to first sc.

Note: Loop a short piece of yarn around any stitch to mark Rnd 1 as **right** side.

Rnd 2: Ch 1, 2 sc in each sc around; join with slip st to first sc: 12 sc.

Rnd 3: Ch 1, 2 sc in same st as joining, sc in next sc, (2 sc in next sc, sc in next sc) around; join with slip st to first sc: 18 sc.

Rnd 4: Ch 1, sc in same st as joining and in next sc, 2 sc in next sc, (sc in next 2 sc, 2 sc in next sc) around; join with slip st to first sc: 24 sc.

Rnd 5: Ch 1, sc in same st as joining, 2 sc in next sc, (sc in next 3 sc, 2 sc in next sc) around to last 2 sc, sc in last 2 sc; join with slip st to first sc, finish off: 30 sc.

SIDES

Note: You can make any flavor of soda. We used Dk Purple and also Red for a Cola.

Rnd 1: With **right** side facing and working in Back Loops Only *(Fig. 1, page 95)*, join desired color with sc in same st as joining on Bottom *(see Joining With Sc, page 95)*; sc in next sc and in each sc around; join with slip st to **both** loops of first sc.

Rnds 2-10: Ch 1, sc in both loops of each sc around; join with slip st to first sc.

Rnd 11: Ch 1, beginning in same st as joining, (sc2tog, sc in next 3 sc) around; join with slip st to first sc: 24 sc.

Rnd 12: Ch 1, sc in each sc around; join with slip st to first sc, finish off.

Finished Size: Approximately 1¹/₂" diameter x 2" high (4 cm x 5 cm)

Yarn Colors

Soda
- ☐ Grey
- ☐ Dk Purple
- ☐ Blue
- ☐ Lt Pink

Cola
- ☐ Grey
- ☐ Red
- ☐ Black

TOP

Work same as Bottom through Rnd 4: 24 sc.

Finish off leaving a long end for sewing.

Using photo as a guide for placement:

Soda: With Lt Pink, embroider "Soda" on the side of the can across Rnds 6-9 using straight stitch *(Fig. 7, page 96)*.
With Blue, embroider a line to indicate the label using backstitch *(Fig. 6, page 96)*.

Cola: With Black, embroider "Cola" on the side of the can across Rnds 6-8 using straight stitch *(Fig. 7, page 96)*.

Stuff the can with polyester fiberfill.

Whipstitch Rnd 4 of the Top to Rnd 12 of the Sides *(Fig. 4a, page 96)*.

Finished Size: Approximately 1¹/₂" diameter x 2" high (4 cm x 5 cm)

Yarn Colors

- ☐ Grey
- ☐ Dk Green
- ☐ White
- ☐ Lime Green
- ☐ Dk Grey

BOTTOM

Work same as Soda & Cola.

SIDES

Using Dk Green, work same as Soda & Cola.

TOP

Work same as Soda & Cola Bottom through Rnd 4: 24 sc.

Finish off leaving a long end for sewing.

LABEL

With White, work same as Soda & Cola Bottom through Rnd 4: 24 sc.

Finish off leaving a long end for sewing.

Using photo as a guide for placement:
With Dk Grey, embroider "Beer" on the Label across Rnds 3 and 4 using straight stitch *(Fig. 7, page 96)*.
With Lime Green, embroider lines for decoration using backstitch *(Fig. 6, page 96)*.

Whipstitch the Label to the Sides *(Figs. 4a & b, page 96)*.

Stuff the can with polyester fiberfill.

Whipstitch Rnd 4 of the Top to Rnd 12 of the Sides.

Finished Size: Approximately 2½" wide x 2¾" high (6.5 cm x 7 cm)

Yarn Colors

- ☐ Orange
- ☐ Lt Yellow
- ☐ Dk Brown
- ☐ White

JUG

With Orange, ch 9.

Rnd 1 (Right side): Sc in second ch from hook and in next 6 chs, 3 sc in last ch; working in free loops of beginning ch *(Fig. 2b, page 95)*, sc in next 6 chs, 2 sc in next ch; join with slip st to first sc: 18 sc.

Rnd 2: Ch 1, 2 sc in same st as joining, sc in next 6 sc, 2 sc in each of next 3 sc, sc in next 6 sc, 2 sc in each of last 2 sc; join with slip st to first sc: 24 sc.

Rnd 3: Ch 1, 2 sc in same st as joining, sc in next 7 sc, 2 sc in next sc, (sc in next sc, 2 sc in next sc) twice, sc in next 7 sc, (2 sc in next sc, sc in next sc) twice; join with slip st to first sc: 30 sc.

Rnd 4: Ch 1, 2 sc in same st as joining, sc in next 8 sc, 2 sc in next sc, (sc in next 2 sc, 2 sc in next sc) twice, sc in next 8 sc, (2 sc in next sc, sc in next 2 sc) twice; join with slip st to first sc: 36 sc.

Rnd 5: Ch 1, 2 sc in same st as joining, sc in next 9 sc, 2 sc in next sc, (sc in next 3 sc, 2 sc in next sc) twice, sc in next 9 sc, (2 sc in next sc, sc in next 3 sc) twice; join with slip st to first sc: 42 sc.

Rnd 6: Ch 1, sc in Back Loop Only of each sc around *(Fig. 1, page 95)*; join with slip st to **both** loops of first sc.

Rnds 7-11: Ch 1, sc in both loops of each sc around; join with slip st to first sc.

Finish off.

Rnd 12: With **right** side facing, skip first 26 sc and join Orange with slip st in next sc; ch 1, beginning in same st as joining, sc2tog, sc in next 11 sc, sc2tog twice, sc in next 12 sc, sc2tog, leave remaining 11 sc unworked for Handle; join with slip st to first sc: 27 sc.

Rnd 13: Ch 1, beginning in same st as joining, sc2tog, sc in each sc around to last 2 sc, sc2tog; join with slip st to first sc: 25 sc.

Rnds 14 and 15: Ch 1, sc in each sc around; join with slip st to first sc.

Rnd 16: Ch 1, 2 sc in same st as joining and in next sc, sc in each sc around to last 2 sc, 2 sc in each of last 2 sc; join with slip st to first sc, finish off: 29 sc.

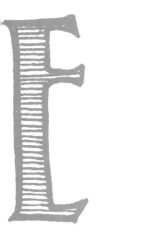 

HANDLE

Rnd 1: With **right** side facing, join Orange with slip st in first unworked sc on Rnd 11; ch 1, beginning in same st as joining, sc2tog, sc in next 7 sc, sc2tog; join with slip st to first sc: 9 sc.

Stuff the Jug with polyester fiberfill; stuff the Handle as you work.

Rnds 2-4: Ch 1, sc in each sc around; join with slip st to first sc.

Rnd 5: Ch 1, 2 sc in same st as joining, sc in next 7 sc, 2 sc in last sc; join with slip st to first sc, do **not** finish off: 11 sc.

TOP

Rnd 1: Ch 1, sc in each sc around Handle and Jug; join with slip st to first sc: 40 sc.

Rnd 2: Ch 1, beginning in same st as joining, (sc2tog, sc in next 2 sc) around; join with slip st to first sc: 30 sc.

Rnd 3: Ch 1, sc in same st as joining, sc2tog, (sc in next sc, sc2tog) around; join with slip st to first sc: 20 sc.

Rnd 4: Ch 1, beginning in same st as joining, sc2tog around; join with slip st to first sc, finish off: 10 sc.

Stuff the Top with polyester fiberfill.

CAP

Rnd 1: With **right** side facing, join Lt Yellow with sc in first sc *(see Joining With Sc, page 95)*; sc in next sc and in each sc around; join with slip st to first sc.

Rnd 2: Ch 1, sc in each sc around; join with slip st to first sc.

Rnd 3: Ch 1, working in Back Loops Only and beginning in same st as joining, sc2tog around; join with slip st to **both** loops of first sc, finish off leaving a long end for sewing: 5 sc.

Weave end through remaining sc *(Fig. 5, page 96)*; gather tightly to close and secure end.

Using photo as a guide for placement:
With Dk Brown, embroider "JUICE" across Rnds 11 and 12 using straight stitch *(Fig. 7, page 96)*.

With White, embroider a line to indicate the label using backstitch *(Fig. 6, page 96)*.

FRUIT

Fruit is a natural choice for snacking. Pick Bananas, Starfruit, Mangosteen, Pear, Persimmon, and Watermelon.

 **EASY**

Shopping List

Yarn (Fine Weight)

Note: Light or Medium Weight yarn can be used, but the finished sizes will be slightly larger *(see Getting Started, page 4)*. See individual project for colors needed.

Crochet Hook

☐ Steel, size 2 (2.25 mm) **or** aluminum size B (2.25 mm) **or** size needed to achieve a dense gauge

Additional Supplies

☐ Tapestry needle
☐ Polyester fiberfill

GAUGE INFORMATION

Use the size hook needed to achieve a dense gauge *(see Crochet Hook Size & Gauge, page 5)*.

STITCH GUIDE

SINGLE CROCHET 2 TOGETHER *(abbreviated sc2tog)*
Pull up a loop in each of next 2 sc, YO and draw through all 3 loops on hook **(counts as one sc)**.

BANANAS

Finished Size: Approximately 1³/₄" diameter x 3" long (4.5 cm x 7.5 cm)

Yarn Colors
- ☐ Yellow
- ☐ Black

STEM
With Yellow, ch 4; join with slip st to form a ring.

Rnd 1 (Right side): Ch 1, 6 sc in ring; join with slip st to first sc.

Rnd 2: Ch 1, 2 sc in each sc around; join with slip st to first sc: 12 sc.

Rnds 3-10: Ch 1, sc in each sc around; join with slip st to first sc.

Stuff the Stem with polyester fiberfill.

Rnd 11: Ch 1, beginning in same st as joining, sc2tog around; join with slip st to first sc: 6 sc.

Rnd 12: Ch 1, sc in each sc around; join with slip st to first sc, finish off leaving a long end for sewing.

Weave end through remaining sc *(Fig. 5, page 96)*; gather tightly to close and secure end.

BANANA (Make 2)
With Black, ch 4; join with slip st to form a ring.

Rnd 1 (Right side): Ch 1, 6 sc in ring; cut Black, with Yellow join with slip st to first sc *(Fig. 3c, page 96)*.

Rnd 2: Ch 1, 2 sc in same st as joining, sc in next sc, (2 sc in next sc, sc in next sc) twice; join with slip st to first sc: 9 sc.

Rnd 3: Ch 1, sc in same st as joining and in next sc, 2 sc in next sc, (sc in next 2 sc, 2 sc in next sc) around; join with slip st to first sc: 12 sc.

nd 4: Ch 1, sc in same st as joining, 2 sc
n next sc, (sc in next 3 sc, 2 sc in next sc)
wice, sc in last 2 sc; join with slip st to first
c: 15 sc.

nds 5-13: Ch 1, sc in each sc around; join
ith slip st to first sc.

tuff the Banana with polyester fiberfill as
ou work.

nd 14: Ch 1, sc in same st as joining and
n next sc, sc2tog, (sc in next 3 sc, sc2tog)
wice, sc in last sc; join with slip st to first
c: 12 sc.

nd 15: Ch 1, beginning in same st as
oining, (sc2tog, sc in next 2 sc) around;
oin with slip st to first sc: 9 sc.

nd 16: Ch 1, beginning in same st as
oining, (sc2tog, sc in next sc) around; join
ith slip st to first sc: 6 sc.

nds 17 and 18: Ch 1, sc in each sc
round; join with slip st to first sc.

inish off leaving a long end for sewing.

Ising photo as a guide for placement,
whipstitch the last rnd of both Bananas
o the side of the Stem *(Figs. 4a & b,*
age 96).

STARFRUIT

Finished Size: Approximately 2" (5 cm) diameter

Yarn Color
☐ Chartreuse

WEDGE (Make 5)
With Chartreuse, ch 17.

Rnd 1 (Right side)**:** Sc in second ch from hook, hdc in next ch, dc in
next 12 chs, hdc in next ch, 3 sc in last ch; working in free loops of
beginning ch *(Fig. 2b, page 95)*, hdc in next ch, dc in next 12 chs, hdc
in next ch, 2 sc in next ch; join with slip st to first sc: 34 sts.

Note: Loop a short piece of yarn around any stitch to mark Rnd 1 as
right side.

Rnd 2: Ch 1, sc in same st as joining, hdc in next hdc, dc in next
12 dc, hdc in next hdc, sc in next 3 sc, hdc in next hdc, dc in next
12 dc, hdc in next hdc, sc in last 2 sc; join with slip st to first sc,
finish off leaving a long end for sewing.

Matching sts and beginning in center sc of 3-sc group on either end,
whipstitch the Wedges together *(Fig. 4a, page 96)*, forming a circle
and stuffing the Starfruit with polyester fiberfill before closing.

MANGOSTEEN

Finished Size: Approximately 1¼" diameter x 1½" high (3 cm x 4 cm)

Yarn Colors
- ☐ Dk Purple
- ☐ Green

BODY

With Dk Purple, ch 4; join with slip st to form a ring.

Rnd 1 (Right side)**:** Ch 1, 6 sc in ring; join with slip st to first sc.

Rnd 2: Ch 1, 2 sc in each sc around; join with slip st to first sc: 12 sc.

Rnd 3: Ch 1, 2 sc in same st as joining, sc in next sc, (2 sc in next sc, sc in next sc) around; join with slip st to first sc: 18 sc.

Rnd 4: Ch 1, sc in same st as joining and in next sc, 2 sc in next sc, (sc in next 2 sc, 2 sc in next sc) around; join with slip st to first sc: 24 sc.

Rnds 5-7: Ch 1, sc in each sc around; join with slip st to first sc.

Stuff the Mangosteen with polyester fiberfill as you work.

Rnd 8: Ch 1, beginning in same st as joining, (sc2tog, sc in next 2 sc) around; join with slip st to first sc: 18 sc.

Rnd 9: Ch 1, sc in same st as joining, sc2tog, (sc in next sc, sc2tog) around; join with slip st to first sc: 12 sc.

Rnd 10: Ch 1, beginning in same st as joining, sc2tog around; join with slip st to first sc, finish off: 6 sc.

STEM & LEAVES

With Green, ch 4; join with slip st to form a ring.

Rnd 1 (Right side)**:** Ch 1, 6 sc in ring; join with slip st to first sc.

Rnd 2: Ch 1, sc in Back Loop Only of each sc around *(Fig. 1, page 95)*; join with slip st to **both** loops of first sc.

Rnd 3: Ch 1, sc in both loops of each sc around; join with slip st to first sc.

Rnd 4: Ch 1, 2 sc in each sc around; join with slip st to first sc: 12 sc.

Rnd 5: ★ Ch 2, 2 dc in next sc, ch 2, slip st in next sc; repeat from ★ around working last slip st in joining st; finish off leaving a long end for sewing.

Sew the Leaves to the top of the Mangosteen.

PEAR

Finished Size: Approximately 1½" diameter x 2" high (4 cm x 5 cm)

Yarn Colors
- ☐ Lt Green
- ☐ Brown

BODY

With Lt Green, ch 4; join with slip st to form a ring.

Rnd 1 (Right side)**:** Ch 1, 6 sc in ring; join with slip st to first sc.

Rnd 2: Ch 1, 2 sc in each sc around; join with slip st to first sc: 12 sc.

Rnd 3: Ch 1, 2 sc in same st as joining, sc in next sc, (2 sc in next sc, sc in next sc) around; join with slip st to first sc: 18 sc.

Rnd 4: Ch 1, sc in same st as joining and in next sc, 2 sc in next sc, (sc in next 2 sc, 2 sc in next sc) around; join with slip st to first sc: 24 sc.

Rnd 5: Ch 1, sc in same st as joining, 2 sc in next sc, (sc in next 3 sc, 2 sc in next sc) around to last 2 sc, sc in last 2 sc; join with slip st to first sc: 30 sc.

Rnds 6-9: Ch 1, sc in each sc around; join with slip st to first sc.

Rnd 10: Ch 1, sc in same st as joining and in next 2 sc, sc2tog, (sc in next 3 sc, sc2tog) around; join with slip st to first sc: 24 sc.

Rnd 11: Ch 1, sc in same st as joining, sc2tog, (sc in next 2 sc, sc2tog) around to last sc, sc in last sc; join with slip st to first sc: 18 sc.

Rnds 12-14: Ch 1, sc in each sc around; join with slip st to first sc.

Stuff the Pear with polyester fiberfill.

Rnd 15: Ch 1, beginning in same st as joining, (sc2tog, sc in next sc) around; join with slip st to first sc: 12 sc.

Rnd 16: Ch 1, beginning in same st as joining, sc2tog around; join with slip st to first sc, finish off leaving a long end for sewing: 6 sc.

STEM

With Brown, ch 10; finish off.

Insert the Stem into the top of the Pear and tack in place with Lt Green end.

PERSIMMON

Finished Size: Approximately 1¹/₂"
diameter x 1" high (4 cm x 2.5 cm)

Yarn Colors
- ☐ Orange
- ☐ Brown

With Orange, ch 4; join with slip st to form a ring.

Rnd 1 (Right side): Ch 1, 6 sc in ring; join with slip st to first sc.

Rnd 2: Ch 1, 2 sc in each sc around; join with slip st to first sc: 12 sc.

Rnd 3: Ch 1, 2 sc in same st as joining, sc in next sc, (2 sc in next sc, sc in next sc) around; join with slip st to first sc: 18 sc.

Rnd 4: Ch 1, sc in same st as joining and in next sc, 2 sc in next sc, (sc in next 2 sc, 2 sc in next sc) around; join with slip st to first sc: 24 sc.

Rnd 5: Ch 1, sc in same st as joining, 2 sc in next sc, (sc in next 3 sc, 2 sc in next sc) around to last 2 sc, sc in last 2 sc; join with slip st to first sc: 30 sc.

Rnds 6 and 7: Ch 1, sc in each sc around; join with slip st to first sc.

Rnd 8: Ch 1, sc in same st as joining and in next 2 sc, sc2tog, (sc in next 3 sc, sc2tog) around; join with slip st to first sc: 24 sc.

Stuff the Persimmon with polyester fiberfill as you work.

Rnd 9: Ch 1, sc in same st as joining, sc2tog, (sc in next 2 sc, sc2tog) around to last sc, sc in last sc; join with slip st to first sc: 18 sc.

Rnd 10: Ch 1, beginning in same st as joining, (sc2tog, sc in next sc) around; join with slip st to first sc: 12 sc.

Rnd 11: Ch 1, beginning in same st as joining, sc2tog around; join with slip st to first sc, finish off: 6 sc.

LEAVES
With Brown, ch 4; join with slip st to form a ring.

Rnd 1 (Right side): Ch 1, 6 sc in ring; join with slip st to first sc.

Rnd 2: (Ch 3, slip st in next sc) around, working last slip st in same st as joining; finish off leaving a long end for sewing: 6 ch-3 sps.

Sew the Leaves to the top of the Persimmon.

Finished Size: Approximately 2³/₄"
diameter x 1³/₄" high (7 cm x 4.5 cm)

Yarn Colors
- ☐ Green
- ☐ Red
- ☐ White
- ☐ Dk Green
- ☐ Black

RIND

With Green, ch 4; join with slip st to form a ring.

Rnd 1 (Right side): Ch 1, 6 sc in ring; join with slip st to first sc.

Note: Loop a short piece of yarn around any stitch to mark Rnd 1 as **right** side.

Rnd 2: Ch 1, 2 sc in each sc around; join with slip st to first sc: 12 sc.

WATERMELON

Rnd 3: Ch 1, 2 sc in same st as joining, sc in next sc, (2 sc in next sc, sc in next sc) around; join with slip st to first sc: 18 sc.

Rnd 4: Ch 1, sc in same st as joining and in next sc, 2 sc in next sc, (sc in next 2 sc, 2 sc in next sc) around; join with slip st to first sc: 24 sc.

Rnd 5: Ch 1, sc in same st as joining, 2 sc in next sc, (sc in next 3 sc, 2 sc in next sc) around to last 2 sc, sc in last 2 sc; join with slip st to first sc: 30 sc.

Rnd 6: Ch 1, sc in same st as joining and in next 3 sc, 2 sc in next sc, (sc in next 4 sc, 2 sc in next sc) around; join with slip st to first sc: 36 sc.

Rnd 7: Ch 1, sc in same st as joining and in next sc, 2 sc in next sc, (sc in next 5 sc, 2 sc in next sc) around to last 3 sc, sc in last 3 sc; join with slip st to first sc: 42 sc.

Rnd 8: Ch 1, sc in same st as joining and in next 5 sc, 2 sc in next sc, (sc in next 6 sc, 2 sc in next sc) around; join with slip st to first sc: 48 sc.

Rnd 9: Ch 1, sc in same st as joining and in next sc, 2 sc in next sc, (sc in next 7 sc, 2 sc in next sc) around to last 5 sc, sc in last 5 sc; join with slip st to first sc: 54 sc.

Rnds 10-14: Ch 1, sc in each sc around; join with slip st to first sc.

Finish off.

FLESH
With Red, work same as Rind through Rnd 7: 42 sc.

Rnd 8: Ch 1, sc in same st as joining and in next 5 sc, 2 sc in next sc, (sc in next 6 sc, 2 sc in next sc) around; cut Red, with White, join with slip st to first sc *(Fig. 3c, page 96)*: 48 sc.

Rnd 9: Ch 1, sc in same st as joining and in next sc, 2 sc in next sc, (sc in next 7 sc, 2 sc in next sc) around to last 5 sc, sc in last 5 sc; join with slip st to first sc, finish off leaving a long end for sewing: 54 sc.

Using photo as a guide for placement:
With Dk Green, embroider zigzag lines on the Rind using straight stitch *(Fig. 7, page 96)*.

With Black, embroider seeds on the Flesh using straight stitch.

Whipstitch Rnd 9 of the Flesh to Rnd 14 of the Rind, stuffing the Watermelon with polyester fiberfill before closing.

MEALS

For lunch or dinner, popular choices include Hamburger, Meatball Spaghetti, and Pepperoni Pizza.

 **EASY**

Shopping List

Yarn (Fine Weight)
Note: Light or Medium Weight yarn can be used, but the finished sizes will be slightly larger *(see Getting Started, page 4)*. See individual project for colors needed.

Crochet Hook
- [ ] Steel, size 2 (2.25 mm) **or** aluminum size B (2.25 mm)
  or size needed to achieve a dense gauge

Additional Supplies
- [ ] Tapestry needle
- [ ] Polyester fiberfill
- [ ] Optional: Craft glue

GAUGE INFORMATION

Use the size hook needed to achieve a dense gauge *(see Crochet Hook Size & Gauge, page 5)*.

——— STITCH GUIDE ———

SINGLE CROCHET 2 TOGETHER *(abbreviated sc2tog)*
Pull up a loop in each of next 2 sc, YO and draw through all 3 loops on hook (**counts as one sc**).

HAMBURGER

Shown with Small Plate, page 88.

Finished Size: Approximately 1³/₄"
diameter x 2" high (4.5 cm x 5 cm)

Yarn Colors
- ☐ Tan
- ☐ Brown
- ☐ Green
- ☐ Yellow

BUN (Make 2)
With Tan, ch 4; join with slip st to
form a ring.

Rnd 1 (Right side)**:** Ch 1, 6 sc in ring;
join with slip st to first sc.

Rnd 2: Ch 1, 2 sc in each sc around;
join with slip st to first sc: 12 sc.

Rnd 3: Ch 1, 2 sc in same st as
joining, sc in next sc, (2 sc in next sc,
sc in next sc) around; join with slip st
to first sc: 18 sc.

Rnd 4: Ch 1, sc in same st as joining
and in next sc, 2 sc in next sc, (sc in
next 2 sc, 2 sc in next sc) around; join
with slip st to first sc: 24 sc.

Rnd 5: Ch 1, sc in same st as joining,
2 sc in next sc, (sc in next 3 sc, 2 sc in
next sc) around to last 2 sc, sc in last
2 sc; join with slip st to first sc: 30 sc.

Rnd 6: Ch 1, sc in each sc around;
join with slip st to first sc.

Rnd 7: Ch 1, working in Back Loops
Only *(Fig. 1, page 95)*, sc in same st
as joining and in next 2 sc, sc2tog,
(sc in next 3 sc, sc2tog) around; join
with slip st to **both** loops of first sc:
24 sc.

Rnd 8: Ch 1, sc in same st as joining,
sc2tog, (sc in next 2 sc, sc2tog)
around to last sc, sc in last sc; join
with slip st to first sc: 18 sc.

Stuff the Bun lightly with polyester
fiberfill as you work.

Rnd 9: Ch 1, beginning in same st
as joining, (sc2tog, sc in next sc)
around; join with slip st to first sc:
12 sc.

Rnd 10: Ch 1, beginning in same st
as joining, sc2tog around; join with
slip st to first sc, finish off leaving a
long end for sewing: 6 sc.

Weave end through remaining sc
(Fig. 5, page 96); gather tightly to
close and secure end.

BURGER

With Brown, work same as Bun, working in both loops throughout (including Rnd 7), without stuffing.

LETTUCE

With Green, work same as Bun through Rnd 4: 24 sc.

Rnd 5: Ch 5, (dc, ch 2) 3 times in same st as joining, (dc, ch 2) 4 times in next sc and in each sc around; join with slip st to third ch of beginning ch-5, finish off.

CHEESE

With Yellow, ch 11.

Row 1: Sc in second ch from hook and in each ch across: 10 sc.

Rows 2-10: Ch 1, turn; sc in each sc across.

Finish off.

Stack all of the pieces in any order and using Tan, sew through the center of each piece to hold them together.

MEATBALL

Spaghetti

Shown with Bowl, page 92.

Finished Size: Approximately 2¹/₂" diameter x 1" high (6.5 cm x 2.5 cm) in Bowl

Yarn Colors
- ☐ Lt Yellow
- ☐ Brown

NOODLE (Make 8)

With Lt Yellow, ch 50; finish off.

MEATBALL (Make 6)

With Brown, ch 4; join with slip st to form a ring.

Rnd 1 (Right side)**:** Ch 1, 6 sc in ring; join with slip st to first sc.

Rnd 2: Ch 1, sc in each sc around; join with slip st to first sc, finish off.

Using photo as a guide, place the Noodles and Meatballs in a Bowl or on a plate, arranging them to look like spaghetti; tack or glue them in place if desired.

PEPPERONI PIZZA

Shown with Extra Large Plate, page 84.

Finished Size: Approximately 3¹/₄" (8.5 cm) diameter

Yarn Colors
- ☐ Lt Yellow
- ☐ Tan
- ☐ Dk Red

PIZZA PIE
CHEESE

With Lt Yellow, ch 4; join with slip st to form a ring.

Row 1 (Right side): Ch 1, 5 sc in ring; do **not** join.

Note: Loop a short piece of yarn around any stitch to mark Row 1 as **right** side.

Row 2: Ch 1, turn; 2 sc in each sc across: 10 sc.

Row 3: Ch 1, turn; 2 sc in first sc, sc in next sc, (2 sc in next sc, sc in next sc) across: 15 sc.

Row 4: Ch 1, turn; 2 sc in first sc, sc in next 2 sc, (2 sc in next sc, sc in next 2 sc) across: 20 sc.

Row 5: Ch 1, turn; 2 sc in first sc, sc in next 3 sc, (2 sc in next sc, sc in next 3 sc) across: 25 sc.

Row 6: Ch 1, turn; 2 sc in first sc, sc in next 4 sc, (2 sc in next sc, sc in next 4 sc) across: 30 sc.

Row 7: Ch 1, turn; 2 sc in first sc, sc in next 5 sc, (2 sc in next sc, sc in next 5 sc) across: 35 sc.

Row 8: Ch 1, turn; 2 sc in first sc, sc in next 6 sc, (2 sc in next sc, sc in next 6 sc) across: 40 sc.

Row 9: Ch 1, turn; 2 sc in first sc, (sc in next 7 sc, 2 sc in next sc) across to last 7 sc, sc in last 7 sc changing to Tan in last sc made *(Fig. 3a, page 96)*, cut Lt Yellow: 45 sc.

CRUST

Row 1: Ch 1, turn; 2 sc in first sc, sc in next 8 sc, (2 sc in next sc, sc in next 8 sc) across: 50 sc.

Row 2: Ch 1, turn; sc in each sc across.

Row 3: Ch 1, turn; beginning in first sc, (sc2tog, sc in next 8 sc) across: 45 sc.

Row 4: Ch 1, turn; beginning in first sc, (sc2tog, sc in next 7 sc) across: 40 sc.

Row 5: Ch 1, turn; beginning in first sc, (sc2tog, sc in next 6 sc) across: 35 sc.

Row 6: Ch 1, turn; beginning in first sc, (sc2tog, sc in next 5 sc) across: 30 sc.

Row 7: Ch 1, turn; beginning in first sc, (sc2tog, sc in next 4 sc) across: 25 sc.

Row 8: Ch 1, turn; beginning in first sc, (sc2tog, sc in next 3 sc) across: 20 sc.

Row 9: Ch 1, turn; beginning in first sc, (sc2tog, sc in next 2 sc) across: 15 sc.

Row 10: Ch 1, turn; beginning in first sc, (sc2tog, sc in next sc) across: 10 sc.

Row 11: Ch 1, turn; beginning in first sc, sc2tog across; finish off leaving a long end for sewing: 5 sc.

PIZZA SLICE
CHEESE
Row 1 (Right side)**:** With Lt Yellow, ch 2, 2 sc in second ch from hook.

Note: Mark Row 1 as **right** side.

Row 2: Ch 1, turn; 2 sc in each of 2 sc: 4 sc.

Row 3: Ch 1, turn; 2 sc in first sc, sc in next sc, 2 sc in next sc, sc in last sc: 6 sc.

Row 4: Ch 1, turn; 2 sc in first sc, sc in next 2 sc, 2 sc in next sc, sc in last 2 sc: 8 sc.

Row 5: Ch 1, turn; 2 sc in first sc, sc in next 3 sc, 2 sc in next sc, sc in last 3 sc: 10 sc.

Row 6: Ch 1, turn; 2 sc in first sc, sc in next 4 sc, 2 sc in next sc, sc in last 4 sc: 12 sc.

Row 7: Ch 1, turn; 2 sc in first sc, sc in next 5 sc, 2 sc in next sc, sc in last 5 sc: 14 sc.

Row 8: Ch 1, turn; 2 sc in first sc, sc in next 6 sc, 2 sc in next sc, sc in last 6 sc: 16 sc.

Row 9: Ch 1, turn; 2 sc in first sc, sc in next 7 sc, 2 sc in next sc, sc in last 7 sc changing to Tan in last sc made *(Fig. 3a, page 96)*, cut Lt Yellow: 18 sc.

CRUST
Row 1: Ch 1, turn; 2 sc in first sc, sc in next 8 sc, 2 sc in next sc, sc in last 8 sc: 20 sc.

Row 2: Ch 1, turn; sc in each sc across.

Row 3: Ch 1, turn; beginning in first sc, (sc2tog, sc in next 8 sc) twice: 18 sc.

Row 4: Ch 1, turn; beginning in first sc, (sc2tog, sc in next 7 sc) twice: 16 sc.

Row 5: Ch 1, turn; beginning in first sc, (sc2tog, sc in next 6 sc) twice: 14 sc.

Row 6: Ch 1, turn; beginning in first sc, (sc2tog, sc in next 5 sc) twice: 12 sc.

Row 7: Ch 1, turn; beginning in first sc, (sc2tog, sc in next 4 sc) twice: 10 sc.

Row 8: Ch 1, turn; beginning in first sc, (sc2tog, sc in next 3 sc) twice: 8 sc.

Row 9: Ch 1, turn; beginning in first sc, (sc2tog, sc in next 2 sc) twice: 6 sc.

Row 10: Ch 1, turn; beginning in first sc, (sc2tog, sc in next sc) twice: 4 sc.

Row 11: Ch 1, turn; beginning in first sc, sc2tog twice; finish off leaving a long end for sewing: 2 sc.

PEPPERONI (Make 10)
With Dk Red, ch 4; join with slip st to form a ring.

Rnd 1 (Right side)**:** Ch 1, 7 sc in ring; join with slip st to first sc, finish off leaving a long end for sewing.

Using photo as a guide for placement, sew 7 Pepperoni to Pizza Pie and 3 Pepperoni to Pizza Slice.

Flatten Pizza Pie with **wrong** sides together and whipstitch end of rows of the Cheese and the Crust together *(Fig. 4a, page 96)*. Repeat for Pizza Slice.

MEATS

The best meals revolve around delicious meats, such as Fish, Ham, Sausage Links, Sushi, and Turkey.

 EASY

Shopping List

Yarn (Fine Weight)

Note: Light or Medium Weight yarn can be used, but the finished sizes will be slightly larger *(see Getting Started, page 4)*. See individual project for colors needed.

Crochet Hook

☐ Steel, size 2 (2.25 mm) **or** aluminum size B (2.25 mm)

☐ **or** size needed to achieve a dense gauge

Additional Supplies

☐ Tapestry needle

☐ Polyester fiberfill

GAUGE INFORMATION

Use the size hook needed to achieve a dense gauge *(see Crochet Hook Size & Gauge, page 5)*.

——— STITCH GUIDE ———

SINGLE CROCHET 2 TOGETHER *(abbreviated sc2tog)*

Pull up a loop in each of next 2 sc, YO and draw through all 3 loops on hook **(counts as one sc)**.

FISH

Finished Size: Approximately 2³/₄" long x 2" wide (7 cm x 5 cm)

Yarn Colors
- ☐ Grey
- ☐ Dk Grey

BODY

With Grey, ch 4; join with slip st to form a ring.

Rnd 1 (Right side)**:** Ch 1, 6 sc in ring; join with slip st to first sc.

Rnd 2: Ch 1, 2 sc in each sc around; join with slip st to first sc: 12 sc.

Rnd 3: Ch 1, 2 sc in same st as joining, sc in next 5 sc, 2 sc in next sc, sc in last 5 sc; join with slip st to first sc: 14 sc.

Rnd 4: Ch 1, 2 sc in same st as joining, sc in next 6 sc, 2 sc in next sc, sc in last 6 sc; join with slip st to first sc: 16 sc.

Rnd 5: Ch 1, 2 sc in same st as joining, sc in next 7 sc, 2 sc in next sc, sc in last 7 sc; join with slip st to first sc: 18 sc.

Rnds 6-10: Ch 1, sc in each sc around; join with slip st to first sc.

Rnd 11: Ch 1, beginning in same st as joining, (sc2tog, sc in next 7 sc) twice; join with slip st to first sc: 16 sc.

Stuff the Body with polyester fiberfill as you work.

Rnd 12: Ch 1, beginning in same st as joining, (sc2tog, sc in next 6 sc) twice; join with slip st to first sc: 14 sc.

Rnd 13: Ch 1, beginning in same st as joining, (sc2tog, sc in next 5 sc) twice; join with slip st to first sc: 12 sc.

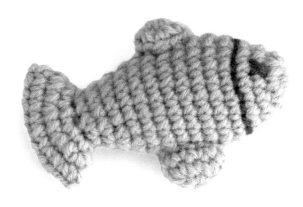

Rnd 14: Ch 1, beginning in same st as joining, (sc2tog, sc in next 4 sc) twice; join with slip st to first sc: 10 sc.

Rnd 15: Ch 1, beginning in same st as joining, (sc2tog, sc in next 3 sc) twice; join with slip st to first sc: 8 sc.

Rnd 16: Ch 1, 2 sc in same st as joining and in next sc, skip next sc, 2 sc in each of last 5 sc; join with slip st to first sc: 14 sc.

Rnd 17: Ch 1, 2 sc in same st as joining, sc in next sc, (2 sc in next sc, sc in next sc) around; join with slip st to first sc: 21 sc.

Rnd 18: Ch 1, sc in each sc around; join with slip st to first sc, finish off leaving a long end for sewing.

Flatten the last rnd and whipstitch the opening closed *(Fig. 4a, page 96)*.

Using photo as a guide for placement:
With Dk Grey, embroider a "X" on Rnd 3 for each eye using straight stitch *(Fig. 7, page 96)*.
With Dk Grey, embroider a line around the head between Rnds 4 and 5 using backstitch *(Fig. 6, page 96)*.

FIN (Make 2)
With Grey, ch 4; join with slip st to form a ring.

Rnd 1 (Right side)**:** Ch 1, 6 sc in ring; join with slip st to first sc.

Rnd 2: Ch 1, 2 sc in same st as joining, sc in next sc, (2 sc in next sc, sc in next sc) twice; join with slip st to first sc, finish off leaving a long end for sewing: 9 sc.

Using photo as a guide for placement, sew the Fins to the Body.

HAM

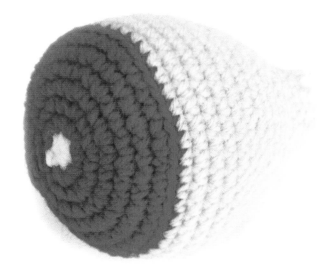

Finished Size: Approximately 2"
diameter x 2³/₄" long (5 cm x 7 cm)

HAM

With White, ch 4; join with slip st to form a ring.

Rnd 1 (Right side)**:** Ch 1, 6 sc in ring; cut White, with Red, join with slip st to first sc *(Fig. 3c, page 96)*.

Rnd 2: Ch 1, 2 sc in each sc around; join with slip st to first sc: 12 sc.

Rnd 3: Ch 1, 2 sc in same st as joining, sc in next sc, (2 sc in next sc, sc in next sc) around; join with slip st to first sc: 18 sc.

Rnd 4: Ch 1, sc in same st as joining and in next sc, 2 sc in next sc, (sc in next 2 sc, 2 sc in next sc) around; join with slip st to first sc: 24 sc.

Rnd 5: Ch 1, sc in same st as joining, 2 sc in next sc, (sc in next 3 sc, 2 sc in next sc) around to last 2 sc, sc in last 2 sc; join with slip st to first sc: 30 sc.

Rnd 6: Ch 1, sc in same st as joining and in next 3 sc, 2 sc in next sc, (sc in next 4 sc, 2 sc in next sc) around; join with slip st to first sc: 36 sc.

Rnd 7: Ch 1, sc in same st as joining and in next sc, 2 sc in next sc, (sc in next 5 sc, 2 sc in next sc) around to last 3 sc, sc in last 3 sc; cut Red, with Ecru, join with slip st to first sc: 42 sc.

Rnd 8: Ch 1, sc in Back Loop Only of each sc around *(Fig. 1, page 95)*; join with slip st to **both** loops of first sc.

Rnds 9-12: Ch 1, sc in both loops of each sc around; join with slip st to first sc.

Rnd 13: Ch 1, sc in same st as joining and in next 4 sc, sc2tog, (sc in next 5 sc, sc2tog) around; join with slip st to first sc: 36 sc.

Rnd 14: Ch 1, sc in each sc around; join with slip st to first sc.

Rnd 15: Ch 1, sc in same st as joining and in next sc, sc2tog, (sc in next 4 sc, sc2tog) around to last 2 sc, sc in last 2 sc; join with slip st to first sc: 30 sc.

Rnd 16: Ch 1, sc in each sc around; join with slip st to first sc.

Rnd 17: Ch 1, sc in same st as joining and in next 2 sc, sc2tog, (sc in next 3 sc, sc2tog) around; join with slip st to first sc: 24 sc.

Rnd 18: Ch 1, sc in each sc around; join with slip st to first sc.

Rnd 19: Ch 1, beginning in same st as joining, (sc2tog, sc in next 2 sc) around; join with slip st to first sc: 18 sc.

Rnd 20: Ch 1, sc in each sc around; join with slip st to first sc.

Stuff the Ham with polyester fiberfill as you work.

Rnd 21: Ch 1, sc in same st as joining, sc2tog, (sc in next sc, sc2tog) around; join with slip st to first sc: 12 sc.

Rnd 22: Ch 1, sc in each sc around; cut Ecru, with White, join with slip st to first sc.

Rnds 23 and 24: Ch 1, sc in each sc around; join with slip st to first sc.

Rnd 25: Ch 1, beginning in same st as joining, sc2tog around; join with slip st to first sc, finish off leaving a long end for sewing: 6 sc.

Weave end through remaining sc *(Fig. 5, page 96)*; gather tightly to close and secure end.

SAUSAGE LINKS

Finished Size: Approximately 1" diameter x 9¼" long (2.5 cm x 23.5 cm)

Yarn Color
☐ Brown

Stuff the Sausage with polyester fiberfill as you work.

SAUSAGE (Make 5)
With Brown, ch 4; join with slip st to form a ring.

Rnd 1 (Right side)**:** Ch 1, 6 sc in ring; join with slip st to first sc.

Rnd 2: Ch 1, 2 sc in each sc around; join with slip st to first sc: 12 sc.

Rnd 3: Ch 1, 2 sc in same st as joining, sc in next sc, (2 sc in next sc, sc in next sc) around; join with slip st to first sc: 18 sc.

Rnds 4-10: Ch 1, sc in each sc around; join with slip st to first sc.

Rnd 11: Ch 1, beginning in same st as joining, (sc2tog, sc in next sc) around; join with slip st to first sc: 12 sc.

Rnd 12: Ch 1, beginning in same st as joining, sc2tog around; join with slip st to first sc, finish off leaving a long end for sewing: 6 sc.

Weave end through remaining sc *(Fig. 5, page 96)*; gather tightly to close and secure end.

String the sausages together, leaving ¼" (.7 cm) strand between them, securing the yarn at the ends of each sausage.

SUSHI

Shown with Small Tray, page 90.

Finished Size: Approximately
¾" high x 1¼" long (2 cm x 3 cm)

Yarn Colors

- ☐ White
- ☐ Orange
- ☐ Yellow
- ☐ Dk Red
- ☐ Olive Green

RICE BALL (Make 3)
With White, ch 4.

Rnd 1 (Right side)**:** Sc in second ch from hook and in next ch, 3 sc in last ch; working in free loops of beginning ch *(Fig. 2b, page 95)*, sc in next ch, 2 sc in next ch; join with slip st to first sc: 8 sc.

Rnd 2: Ch 1, 2 sc in same st as joining, sc in next sc, 2 sc in each of next 3 sc, sc in next sc, 2 sc in each of last 2 sc; join with slip st to first sc: 14 sc.

Rnds 3-6: Ch 1, sc in each sc around; join with slip st to first sc.

Stuff the Rice with polyester fiberfill as you work.

Rnd 7: Ch 1, beginning in same st as joining, sc2tog, sc in next sc, sc2tog 3 times, sc in next sc, sc2tog twice; join with slip st to first sc: 8 sc.

Rnd 8: Ch 1, sc in each sc around; join with slip st to first sc, finish off leaving a long end for sewing.

Flatten Rnd 8 matching the straight edges and whipstitch the opening closed *(Fig. 4a, page 96)*.

TOPPING

Make 1 with Orange (salmon), Yellow (egg), and Dk Red (tuna).

Ch 5.

Rnd 1 (Right side)**:** Sc in second ch from hook and in next 2 chs, 3 sc in last ch; working in free loops of beginning ch, sc in next 2 chs, 2 sc in next ch; join with slip st to first sc: 10 sc.

Rnds 2-9: Ch 1, sc in each sc around; join with slip st to first sc.

Finish off leaving a long end for sewing.

Flatten Rnd 9 matching the straight edges and whipstitch the opening closed.

Using photo as a guide for placement:
With White, embroider diagonal stripes across the Orange Topping using straight stitch *(Fig. 7, page 96)*. Sew each Topping to a Rice Ball.

With Olive Green, ch 21; finish off. Tie the chain around the Yellow Topping and Rice.

TURKEY

Finished Size: Approximately 3¼" wide x 2¾" high (8.5 cm x 7 cm)

Yarn Colors
- ☐ Tan
- ☐ White

BODY

With Tan, ch 9.

Rnd 1 (Right side)**:** Sc in second ch from hook and in next 6 chs, 3 sc in last ch; working in free loops of beginning ch *(Fig. 2b, page 95)*, sc in next 6 chs, 2 sc in next ch; join with slip st to first sc: 18 sc.

Rnd 2: Ch 1, 2 sc in same st as joining, sc in next 6 sc, 2 sc in each of next 3 sc, sc in next 6 sc, 2 sc in each of last 2 sc; join with slip st to first sc: 24 sc.

Rnd 3: Ch 1, 2 sc in same st as joining, sc in next 7 sc, 2 sc in next sc, (sc in next sc, 2 sc in next sc) twice, sc in next 7 sc, (2 sc in next sc, sc in next sc) twice; join with slip st to first sc: 30 sc.

Rnd 4: Ch 1, 2 sc in same st as joining, sc in next 8 sc, 2 sc in next sc, (sc in next 2 sc, 2 sc in next sc) twice, sc in next 8 sc, (2 sc in next sc, sc in next 2 sc) twice; join with slip st to first sc: 36 sc.

Rnds 5-9: Ch 1, sc in each sc around; join with slip st to first sc.

Rnd 10: Ch 1, sc in same st as joining and in next 6 sc, sc2tog, (sc in next 7 sc, sc2tog) around; join with slip st to first sc: 32 sc.

Rnd 11: Ch 1, sc in each sc around; join with slip st to first sc.

Rnd 12: Ch 1, sc in same st as joining and in next 2 sc, sc2tog, (sc in next 6 sc, sc2tog) around to last 3 sc, sc in last 3 sc; join with slip st to first sc: 28 sc.

Rnd 13: Ch 1, sc in each sc around; join with slip st to first sc.

Rnd 14: Ch 1, sc in same st as joining and in next 4 sc, sc2tog, (sc in next 5 sc, sc2tog) around; join with slip st to first sc: 24 sc.

Rnd 15: Ch 1, sc in each sc around; join with slip st to first sc.

Rnd 16: Ch 1, sc in same st as joining, sc2tog, (sc in next 4 sc, sc2tog) around to last 3 sc, sc in last 3 sc; join with slip st to first sc: 20 sc.

Stuff the Body with polyester fiberfill as you work.

Rnd 17: Ch 1, sc in same st as joining and in next 2 sc, sc2tog, (sc in next 3 sc, sc2tog) around; join with slip st to first sc: 16 sc.

Rnd 18: Ch 1, beginning in same st as joining, (sc2tog, sc in next 2 sc) around; join with slip st to first sc: 12 sc.

Rnd 19: Ch 1, sc in same st as joining, sc2tog, (sc in next sc, sc2tog) around; join with slip st to first sc, finish off leaving a long end for sewing: 8 sc.

Flatten the last rnd and whipstitch the opening closed *(Fig. 4a, page 96)*.

LEG (Make 2)
With Tan, ch 4.

Rnd 1 (Right side)**:** Sc in second ch from hook and in next ch, 3 sc in last ch; working in free loops of beginning ch, sc in next ch, 2 sc in next ch; join with slip st to first sc: 8 sc.

Rnd 2: Ch 1, 2 sc in same st as joining, sc in next sc, 2 sc in each of next 3 sc, sc in next sc, 2 sc in each of last 2 sc; join with slip st to first sc: 14 sc.

Rnds 3-5: Ch 1, sc in each sc around; join with slip st to first sc.

Rnd 6: Ch 1, beginning in same st as joining, (sc2tog, sc in next 5 sc) twice; join with slip st to first sc: 12 sc.

Rnd 7: Ch 1, sc in each sc around; join with slip st to first sc.

Stuff the Leg with polyester fiberfill as you work.

Rnd 8: Ch 1, beginning in same st as joining, sc2tog around; join with slip st to first sc: 6 sc.

Rnd 9: Ch 1, sc in each sc around; cut Tan, with White, join with slip st to first sc *(Fig. 3c, page 96)*.

Rnd 10: Ch 1, sc in each sc around; join with slip st to first sc, finish off leaving a long end for sewing.

Weave end through remaining sc *(Fig. 5, page 96)*; gather tightly to close and secure end.

WING (Make 2)
With Tan, ch 4; join with slip st to form a ring.

Rnd 1 (Right side)**:** Ch 1, 6 sc in ring; join with slip st to first sc.

Rnd 2: Ch 1, 2 sc in each sc around; join with slip st to first sc: 12 sc.

Rnd 3: Ch 1, sc in each sc around; join with slip st to first sc.

Rnd 4: Ch 1, beginning in same st as joining, (sc2tog, sc in next sc) around; join with slip st to first sc: 8 sc.

Rnd 5: Ch 1, sc in each sc around; join with slip st to first sc.

Stuff the Wing with polyester fiberfill as you work.

Rnds 6 and 7: Ch 1, sc in same st as joining and in next sc, slip st in next 4 sts, sc in last 2 sc; join with slip st to first sc: 8 sts.

Rnds 8 and 9: Ch 1, sc in each st around; join with slip st to first sc.

Rnd 10: Ch 1, beginning in same st as joining, sc2tog around; join with slip st to first sc: 4 sc.

Rnd 11: Ch 1, sc in each sc around; join with slip st to first sc, finish off.

Using photo as a guide for placement, sew the Legs and Wings to the Body.

SWEETS

For a sweet treat or to top off a meal, present a Cookie, Doughnut, Flan, Gelatin Ring, Lollipops, Strawberry Cake, or Strawberry Cupcake.

■■■□□ EASY

Shopping List

Yarn (Fine Weight)

Note: Light or Medium Weight yarn can be used, but the finished sizes will be slightly larger *(see Getting Started, page 4).* See individual project for colors needed.

Crochet Hook

☐ Steel, size 2 (2.25 mm) **or** aluminum size B (2.25 mm) **or** size needed to achieve a dense gauge

Additional Supplies

☐ Tapestry needle

☐ Polyester fiberfill

☐ Optional: Craft glue

GAUGE INFORMATION

Use the size hook needed to achieve a dense gauge *(see Crochet Hook Size & Gauge, page 5).*

—— STITCH GUIDE ——

SINGLE CROCHET 2 TOGETHER *(abbreviated sc2tog)*

Pull up a loop in each of next 2 sc, YO and draw through all 3 loops on hook **(counts as one sc).**

COOKIE

Shown with Small Plate, page 88.

Finished Size: Approximately 1"
diameter x 3/4" high (2.5 cm x 2 cm)

Yarn Colors
- ☐ Dk Brown
- ☐ White

WAFER (Make 2)
With Dk Brown, ch 4; join with slip st
to form a ring.

Rnd 1 (Right side)**:** Ch 1, 6 sc in ring;
join with slip st to first sc.

Note: Loop a short piece of yarn
around any stitch to mark Rnd 1 as
right side.

Rnd 2: Ch 1, 2 sc in each sc around;
join with slip st to first sc: 12 sc.

Rnd 3: Ch 1, 2 sc in same st as
joining, sc in next sc, (2 sc in next sc,
sc in next sc) around; join with slip st
to first sc: 18 sc.

Rnd 4: Ch 1, sc in each sc around;
join with slip st to first sc.

Rnd 5: Ch 1, beginning in same st as
joining, (sc2tog, sc in next sc) around;
join with slip st to first sc: 12 sc.

Rnd 6: Ch 1, beginning in same st
as joining, sc2tog around; join with
slip st to first sc: 6 sc.

Rnd 7: Ch 1, sc in each sc around;
join with slip st to first sc, finish off.

CREAM FILLING
With White, ch 4; join with slip st to
form a ring.

Rnd 1: Ch 1, 6 sc in ring; join with
slip st to first sc.

Rnd 2: Ch 1, 2 sc in each sc around;
join with slip st to first sc: 12 sc.

Rnd 3: Ch 1, 2 sc in same st as
joining, sc in next sc, (2 sc in next sc,
sc in next sc) around; join with slip st
to first sc, finish off: 18 sc.

Sew or glue the Cream Filling
between both Wafers.

DOUGHNUT

Shown with Medium Tray, page 89.

Finished Size: Approximately 1³/₄" diameter x ¹/₂" high (4.5 cm x 1.2 cm)

Yarn Colors
- ☐ Tan
- ☐ Brown
- ☐ Dk Brown
- ☐ Rose
- ☐ Yellow
- ☐ White

DOUGHNUT

With Tan and leaving a long end for sewing, ch 18; being careful not to twist ch, join with slip st to form a ring.

Rnd 1 (Right side): Ch 1, sc in each ch around; join with slip st to first sc: 18 sc.

Note: Loop a short piece of yarn around any stitch to mark Rnd 1 as **right** side.

Rnd 2: Ch 1, 2 sc in same st as joining, sc in next sc, (2 sc in next sc, sc in next sc) around; join with slip st to first sc: 27 sc.

Rnds 3-6: Ch 1, sc in each sc around; join with slip st to first sc.

Rnd 7: Ch 1, beginning in same st as joining, (sc2tog, sc in next sc) around; join with slip st to first sc: 18 sc.

Rnd 8: Ch 1, sc in each sc around; join with slip st to first sc, finish off.

Matching sts, whipstitch *(Fig. 4a, page 96)* the last rnd to the free loops of the beginning ch *(Fig. 2b, page 95)*, stuffing the Doughnut with polyester fiberfill as you work.

TOPPING

We made one **each** with Dk Brown, Rose, and Yellow.

Using desired color, work same as Doughnut through Rnd 2: 27 sc.

Rnd 3: Ch 1, sc in same st as joining and in next sc, 2 dc in next sc, (sc in next 2 sc, 2 dc in next sc) around; join with slip st to first sc, finish off leaving a long end for sewing: 36 sts.

Using photo as a guide for placement:
With either White, Brown, or desired color, embroider sprinkles on the Topping using straight stitch *(Fig. 7, page 96)*.

Matching the beginning chs, whipstitch the Topping to the Doughnut, then tack Rnd 3 in place.

FLAN

Shown with Dessert Dish, page 91.

Finished Size: Approximately 2" diameter x 1¹/₂" high (5 cm x 4 cm)

Yarn Colors
☐ Dk Brown
☐ Dk Yellow

TOP

With Dk Brown, ch 4; join with slip st to form a ring.

Rnd 1 (Right side): Ch 1, 6 sc in ring; join with slip st to first sc.

Rnd 2: Ch 1, 2 sc in each sc around; join with slip st to first sc: 12 sc.

Rnd 3: Ch 1, 2 sc in same st as joining, sc in next sc, (2 sc in next sc, sc in next sc) around; join with slip st to first sc: 18 sc.

Rnd 4: Ch 1, sc in same st as joining and in next sc, 2 sc in next sc, (sc in next 2 sc, 2 sc in next sc) around; join with slip st to first sc: 24 sc.

Rnd 5: Ch 1, sc in same st as joining, 2 sc in next sc, (sc in next 3 sc, 2 sc in next sc) around to last 2 sc, sc in last 2 sc; cut Dk Brown, with Dk Yellow, join with slip st to first sc *(Fig. 3c, page 96)*: 30 sc.

SIDES

Rnd 1: Ch 1, sc in Back Loop Only of each sc around *(Fig. 1, page 95)*; join with slip st to **both** loops of first sc.

Rnd 2: Ch 1, working in both loops, sc in same st as joining and in next 3 sc, 2 sc in next sc, (sc in next 4 sc, 2 sc in next sc) around; join with slip st to first sc: 36 sc.

Rnd 3: Ch 1, sc in each sc around; join with slip st to first sc.

Rnd 4: Ch 1, sc in same st as joining and in next sc, 2 sc in next sc, (sc in next 5 sc, 2 sc in next sc) around to last 3 sc, sc in last 3 sc; join with slip st to first sc: 42 sc.

Rnd 5: Ch 1, sc in each sc around; join with slip st to first sc, finish off.

BOTTOM

With Dk Yellow, work same as Top through Rnd 4: 24 sc.

Rnd 5: Ch 1, sc in same st as joining, 2 sc in next sc, (sc in next 3 sc, 2 sc in next sc) around to last 2 sc, sc in last 2 sc; join with slip st to first sc: 30 sc.

Rnd 6: Ch 1, sc in same st as joining and in next 3 sc, 2 sc in next sc, (sc in next 4 sc, 2 sc in next sc) around; join with slip st to first sc: 36 sc.

Rnd 7: Ch 1, sc in same st as joining and in next sc, 2 sc in next sc, (sc in next 5 sc, 2 sc in next sc) around to last 3 sc, sc in last 3 sc; join with slip st to first sc, finish off leaving a long end for sewing: 42 sc.

Whipstitch the Bottom to the Sides *(Fig. 4a, page 96)*, stuffing the Flan with polyester fiberfill before closing.

GELATIN RING

Shown with Large Plate, page 86.

Finished Size: Approximately 2¹/₄"
diameter x 1" high (5.5 cm x 2.5 cm)

Yarn Colors
- ☐ Red
- ☐ Orange
- ☐ Yellow
- ☐ Blue
- ☐ Lt Purple
- ☐ Dk Purple

GELATIN RING

With Red, ch 24; being careful not to twist ch, join with slip st to form a ring.

Rnd 1 (Right side)**:** Ch 1, 2 sc in same st as joining, sc in next 3 chs, (2 sc in next ch, sc in next 3 chs) around; join with slip st to first sc: 30 sc.

Rnd 2: Ch 1, sc in same st as joining and in next 2 sc, 2 sc in next sc, (sc in next 4 sc, 2 sc in next sc) around to last sc, sc in last sc; join with slip st to first sc: 36 sc.

Rnd 3: Ch 1, 2 sc in same st as joining, sc in next 5 sc, (2 sc in next sc, sc in next 5 sc) around; join with slip st to first sc: 42 sc.

Rnd 4: Ch 1, sc in same st as joining and in next 2 sc, 2 sc in next sc, (sc in next 6 sc, 2 sc in next sc) around to last 3 sc, sc in last 3 sc; join with slip st to first sc: 48 sc.

Rnd 5: Ch 1, sc in Back Loop Only of each sc around *(Fig. 1, page 95)*; cut Red, with Orange, join with slip st to **both** loops of first sc *(Fig. 3c, page 96)*.

Rnd 6: Ch 1, working in both loops and beginning in same st as joining, (sc2tog, sc in next 6 sc) around; cut Orange, with Yellow, join with slip st to first sc: 42 sc.

Rnd 7: Ch 1, sc in each sc around; cut Yellow, with Blue, join with slip st to first sc.

Rnd 8: Ch 1, sc in same st as joining and in next 2 sc, sc2tog, (sc in next 5 sc, sc2tog) around to last 2 sc, sc in last 2 sc; cut Blue, with Lt Purple, join with slip st to first sc: 36 sc.

Rnd 9: Ch 1, sc in each sc around; cut Lt Purple, with Dk Purple, join with slip st to first sc.

Rnd 10: Ch 1, beginning in same st as joining, (sc2tog, sc in next 4 sc) around; join with slip st to first sc: 30 sc.

Rnd 11: Ch 1, sc in Back Loop Only of each sc around; cut Dk Purple, with Lt Purple, join with slip st to **both** loops of first sc.

Rnd 12: Ch 1, sc in both loops of each sc around; cut Lt Purple, with Blue, join with slip st to first sc.

Rnd 13: Ch 1, sc in each sc around; cut Blue, with Yellow, join with slip st to first sc.

Rnd 14: Ch 1, sc in each sc around; cut Yellow, with Orange, join with slip st to first sc.

Rnd 15: Ch 1, sc in each sc around; cut Orange, with Red, join with slip st to first sc.

Rnd 16: Ch 1, sc in same st as joining and in next sc, sc2tog, (sc in next 3 sc, sc2tog) around to last sc, sc in last sc; join with slip st to first sc, finish off leaving a long end for sewing: 24 sc.

Matching sts, whipstitch *(Fig. 4a, page 96)* the last rnd to the free loops of the beginning ch *(Fig. 2b, page 95)*, stuffing the Ring with polyester fiberfill as you work.

LOLLIPOPS

Ball Lollipop

Finished Size:

Approximately 1¹/₂" wide x 3" long (4 cm x 7.5 cm)

Yarn Colors

☐ Dk Purple
☐ Yellow
☐ Blue
☐ White

CANDY (Make 2)

With Dk Purple, ch 4; join with slip st to form a ring.

Rnd 1 (Right side)**:** Ch 1, 6 sc in ring; join with slip st to first sc.

Note: Loop a short piece of yarn around any stitch to mark Rnd 1 as **right** side.

Rnd 2: Ch 1, 2 sc in each sc around; cut Dk Purple, with Yellow, join with slip st to first sc *(Fig. 3c, page 96)*: 12 sc.

Rnd 3: Ch 1, 2 sc in same st as joining, sc in next sc, (2 sc in next sc, sc in next sc) around; join with slip st to first sc: 18 sc.

Rnd 4: Ch 1, sc in same st as joining and in next sc, 2 sc in next sc, (sc in next 2 sc, 2 sc in next sc) around; cut Yellow, with Blue, join with slip st to first sc: 24 sc.

Rnd 5: Ch 1, sc in same st as joining, 2 sc in next sc, (sc in next 3 sc, 2 sc in next sc) around to last 2 sc, sc in last 2 sc; join with slip st to first sc: 30 sc.

Rnd 6: Ch 1, sc in each sc around; join with slip st to first sc, finish off leaving a long end for sewing on one of the pieces.

With **wrong** sides together, whipstitch both pieces together *(Fig. 4a, page 96)*, stuffing the Candy with polyester fiberfill before closing.

STICK

With White, ch 4; join with slip st to form a ring.

Rnd 1 (Right side)**:** Ch 1, 6 sc in ring; join with slip st to first sc.

Rnds 2-8: Ch 1, sc in each sc around; join with slip st to first sc.

Finish off leaving a long end for sewing.

Sew Rnd 8 of the Stick to the Candy at the seam.

BALL & PADDLE

Paddle Lollipop

Finished Size: Approximately
1¼" diameter x 2½" high
(3 cm x 6.5 cm)

Yarn Colors
- ☐ Yellow
- ☐ Orange
- ☐ Ecru

CANDY

With Yellow, ch 6.

Rnd 1 (Right side): Sc in second ch from hook and in next 3 chs, 3 sc in last ch; working in free loops of beginning ch (Fig. 2b, page 95), sc in next 3 chs, 2 sc in next ch; join with slip st to first sc: 12 sc.

Rnd 2: Ch 1, 2 sc in same st as joining, sc in next 3 sc, 2 sc in each of next 3 sc, sc in next 3 sc, 2 sc in each of last 2 sc; join with slip st to first sc: 18 sc.

Rnds 3-6: Ch 1, sc in each sc around; join with slip st to first sc.

Rnd 7: Ch 1, sc in each sc around; cut Yellow, with Orange, join with slip st to first sc (Fig. 3c, page 96).

Rnds 8-11: Ch 1, sc in each sc around; join with slip st to first sc.

Stuff the Candy with polyester fiberfill as you work.

Rnd 12: Ch 1, beginning in same st as joining, sc2tog, sc in next 3 sc, sc2tog 3 times, sc in next 3 sc, sc2tog twice; join with slip st to first sc: 12 sc.

Rnd 13: Ch 1, sc in each sc around; join with slip st to first sc, finish off leaving a long end for sewing.

Flatten Rnd 13 matching the straight edges and whipstitch the opening closed (Fig. 4a, page 96).

STICK

With Ecru, ch 4; join with slip st to form a ring.

Rnd 1 (Right side): Ch 1, 6 sc in ring; join with slip st to first sc.

Rnds 2-5: Ch 1, sc in each sc around; join with slip st to first sc.

Finish off leaving a long end for sewing.

Sew Rnd 5 of the Stick to the Candy at the seam.

STRAWBERRY

Finished Size: Approximately 2" wide x 2¾" high (5 cm x 7 cm)

Yarn Colors
- [ ] Lt Pink
- [ ] Rose
- [ ] White
- [ ] Red
- [ ] Olive Green

BOTTOM

With Lt Pink, ch 2.

Row 1: 2 Sc in second ch from hook.

Row 2: Ch 1, turn; 2 sc in each of 2 sc: 4 sc.

Row 3 (Right side)**:** Ch 1, turn; sc in each sc across.

Note: Loop a short piece of yarn around any stitch to mark Row 3 as **right** side.

Row 4: Ch 1, turn; sc in first sc, 2 sc in each of next 2 sc, sc in last sc: 6 sc.

Row 5: Ch 1, turn; sc in each sc across.

Row 6: Ch 1, turn; sc in first sc, 2 sc in next sc, sc in next 2 sc, 2 sc in next sc, sc in last sc: 8 sc.

Row 7: Ch 1, turn; sc in each sc across.

Row 8: Ch 1, turn; sc in first 2 sc, (2 sc in next sc, sc in next 2 sc) twice: 10 sc.

Row 9: Ch 1, turn; sc in each sc across.

Row 10: Ch 1, turn; sc in first 2 sc, 2 sc in next sc, sc in next 4 sc, 2 sc in next sc, sc in last 2 sc: 12 sc.

Row 11: Ch 1, turn; sc in each sc across.

Row 12: Ch 1, turn; sc in first 2 sc, 2 sc in next sc, sc in next 6 sc, 2 sc in next sc, sc in last 2 sc: 14 sc.

Row 13: Ch 1, turn; sc in each sc across.

SIDES

Row 1: Ch 1, do **not** turn; working in end of rows, skip first row, sc in next 12 rows on first side and in first 12 rows on second side, skip last row: 24 sc.

Rows 2-4: Ch 1, turn; sc in each sc across.

Row 5: Ch 1, turn; sc in each sc across to last sc, sc in last sc changing to Rose (*Fig. 3a, page 96*); cut Lt Pink.

Row 6: Ch 1, turn; sc in each sc across to last sc, sc in last sc changing to Lt Pink; cut Rose.

Rows 7-11: Ch 1, turn; sc in each sc across.

Finish off.

CAKE

FROSTING

Row 1: With **right** side facing and working in Back Loops Only on last Row of Bottom *(Fig. 1, page 95)*, and leaving a long end for sewing, join White with sc in first sc *(see Joining With Sc, page 95)*; sc in next sc and in each sc across: 14 sc.

Rows 2-11: Ch 1, turn; sc in both loops of each sc across.

Row 12: Ch 1, turn; sc in Front Loop Only of each sc across.

Row 13: Ch 1, turn; working in both loops, sc in first 2 sc, sc2tog, sc in next 5 sc, sc2tog, sc in last 3 sc: 12 sc.

Row 14: Ch 1, turn; sc in each sc across.

Row 15: Ch 1, turn; sc in first 2 sc, sc2tog, sc in next 4 sc, sc2tog, sc in last 2 sc: 10 sc.

Row 16: Ch 1, turn; sc in each sc across.

Row 17: Ch 1, turn; sc in first 2 sc, (sc2tog, sc in next 2 sc) twice: 8 sc.

Row 18: Ch 1, turn; sc in each sc across.

Row 19: Ch 1, turn; sc in first sc, sc2tog, sc in next 2 sc, sc2tog, sc in last sc: 6 sc.

Row 20: Ch 1, turn; sc in each sc across.

Row 21: Ch 1, turn; sc in first sc, sc2tog twice, sc in last sc: 4 sc.

Row 22: Ch 1, turn; sc in each sc across.

Row 23: Ch 1, turn; beginning in first sc, sc2tog twice: 2 sc.

Row 24: Ch 1, turn; sc2tog; finish off.

Whipstitch the Frosting to the Sides *(Figs. 4a & b, page 96)*, matching Rows 1-11 and stuffing the Cake with polyester fiberfill before closing.

STRAWBERRY

With Red, ch 4; join with slip st to form a ring.

Rnd 1 (Right side)**:** Ch 1, 6 sc in ring; join with slip st to first sc.

Rnd 2: Ch 1, 2 sc in same st as joining, sc in next sc, (2 sc in next sc, sc in next sc) twice; join with slip st to first sc: 9 sc.

Rnd 3: Ch 1, sc in same st as joining and in next sc, 2 sc in next sc, (sc in next 2 sc, 2 sc in next sc) around; join with slip st to first sc: 12 sc.

Rnd 4: Ch 1, sc in same st as joining, 2 sc in next sc, (sc in next 3 sc, 2 sc in next sc) twice, sc in last 2 sc; join with slip st to first sc: 15 sc.

Rnd 5: Ch 1, sc in same st as joining and in next 3 sc, 2 sc in next sc, (sc in next 4 sc, 2 sc in next sc) twice; join with slip st to first sc: 18 sc.

Stuff the Strawberry with polyester fiberfill as you work.

Rnd 6: Ch 1, beginning in same st as joining, (sc2tog, sc in next sc) around; join with slip st to first sc: 12 sc.

Rnd 7: Ch 1, beginning in same st as joining, sc2tog around; join with slip st to first sc, finish off: 6 sc.

LEAF
With Olive Green and leaving a long end for sewing, ch 5; join with slip st to form a ring.

Rnd 1: (Ch 4, slip st in ring) 5 times; finish off.

Sew the Leaf to the top of the Strawberry.

Sew the Strawberry to the top of the Cake.

Finished Size: Approximately 1³/₄" diameter x 2¹/₄" high (4.5 cm x 5.5 cm)

Yarn Colors
- ☐ Tan
- ☐ Lt Pink
- ☐ Red
- ☐ Olive Green

CUPCAKE
With Tan, ch 4; join with slip st to form a ring.

Rnd 1 (Right side): Ch 1, 6 sc in ring; join with slip st to first sc.

Rnd 2: Ch 1, 2 sc in each sc around; join with slip st to first sc: 12 sc.

Rnd 3: Ch 1, 2 sc in same st as joining, sc in next sc, (2 sc in next sc, sc in next sc) around; join with slip st to first sc: 18 sc.

Rnd 4: Ch 1, sc in Back Loop Only of each sc around *(Fig. 1, page 95)*; join with slip st to both loops of first sc.

Rnd 5: Ch 1, working in both loops, sc in same st as joining and in next sc, 2 sc in next sc, (sc in next 2 sc, 2 sc in next sc) around; join with slip st to first sc: 24 sc.

Rnds 6 and 7: Ch 1, sc in each sc around; join with slip st to first sc.

Rnd 8: Ch 1, sc in each sc around; drop Tan, with Lt Pink, join with slip st to first sc *(Fig. 3c, page 96)*.

STRAWBERRY CUPCAKE

Rnd 9: Ch 1, sc in same st as joining and in next sc, 2 sc in next sc, (sc in next 2 sc, 2 sc in next sc) around; join with slip st to first sc: 32 sc.

Rnd 10: Ch 1, sc in same st as joining, 2 sc in next sc, (sc in next 3 sc, 2 sc in next sc) around to last 2 sc, sc in last 2 sc; join with slip st to first sc: 40 sc.

Rnd 11: Ch 1, sc in each sc around; join with slip st to first sc.

Rnd 12: Ch 1, sc in same st as joining and in next 2 sc, sc2tog, (sc in next 3 sc, sc2tog) around; join with slip st to first sc: 32 sc.

Rnd 13: Ch 1, beginning in same st as joining, (sc2tog, sc in next 2 sc) around; join with slip st to first sc: 24 sc.

Rnd 14: Ch 1, sc in same st as joining, sc2tog, (sc in next sc, sc2tog) around; join with slip st to first sc: 16 sc.

Stuff the Cupcake with polyester fiberfill.

Rnd 15: Ch 1, beginning in same st as joining, sc2tog around; join with slip st to first sc: 8 sc.

Rnd 16: Ch 1, sc in each sc around; join with slip st to first sc, finish off leaving a long end for sewing.

STRAWBERRY

Make same as Strawberry Cake, page 69, and sew it to the top of the Cupcake using long Lt Pink end.

·VEGETABLES·

For healthy nourishment, serve plenty of vegetables: Carrot, Corn on the Cob, Cucumber, Eggplant, Lettuce, Potato, Tomato, and Turnip.

◼◼◻◻◻▷ **EASY**

Shopping List

Yarn (Fine Weight)

Note: Light or Medium Weight yarn can be used, but the finished sizes will be slightly larger *(see Getting Started, page 4)*. See individual project for colors needed.

Crochet Hook

☐ Steel, size 2 (2.25 mm) **or** aluminum size B (2.25 mm) **or** size needed to achieve a dense gauge

Additional Supplies

☐ Tapestry needle

☐ Polyester fiberfill

☐ Optional: Craft glue

GAUGE INFORMATION

Use the size hook needed to achieve a dense gauge *(see Crochet Hook Size & Gauge, page 5)*.

——— STITCH GUIDE ———

SINGLE CROCHET 2 TOGETHER *(abbreviated sc2tog)*

Pull up a loop in each of next 2 sc, YO and draw through all 3 loops on hook **(counts as one sc)**.

CARROT

Finished Size: Approximately ¾" diameter x 2" long (2 cm x 5 cm) (excluding Leaves)

Yarn Colors
- [ ] Orange
- [ ] Dk Green

CARROT

With Orange, ch 4; join with slip st to form a ring.

Rnd 1 (Right side): Ch 1, 6 sc in ring; join with slip st to first sc.

Rnd 2: Ch 1, 2 sc in same st as joining, sc in next sc, (2 sc in next sc, sc in next sc) twice; join with slip st to first sc: 9 sc.

Rnd 3: Ch 1, 2 sc in same st as joining, sc in next 2 sc, (2 sc in next sc, sc in next 2 sc) twice; join with slip st to first sc: 12 sc.

Rnd 4: Ch 1, sc in same st as joining, 2 sc in next sc, (sc in next 3 sc, 2 sc in next sc) twice, sc in last 2 sc; join with slip st to first sc: 15 sc.

Rnds 5-13: Ch 1, sc in each sc around; join with slip st to first sc.

Stuff the Carrot with polyester fiberfill as you work.

Rnd 14: Ch 1, beginning in same st as joining, (sc2tog, sc in next 3 sc) 3 times; join with slip st to first sc: 12 sc.

Rnd 15: Ch 1, beginning in same st as joining, sc2tog around; join with slip st to first sc, finish off leaving a long end for sewing: 6 sc.

LEAF (Make 2)
With Dk Green, ch 9.

Row 1: Sc in second ch from hook, hdc in next ch, dc in next 2 chs, hdc in next ch, sc in last 3 chs; finish off: 8 sts.

Insert last stitch made of each Leaf into the top of the Carrot and sew in place using long Orange end.

Finished Size: Approximately 1¼" wide x 2¾" long (3 cm x 7 cm)

Yarn Colors
- [ ] Yellow
- [ ] Lt Green

CORN

With Yellow, ch 4; join with slip st to form a ring.

Rnd 1 (Right side): Ch 1, 6 sc in ring; join with slip st to first sc.

Rnd 2: Ch 1, 2 sc in each sc around; join with slip st to first sc: 12 sc.

Rnd 3: Ch 1, 2 sc in same st as joining, sc in next sc, (2 sc in next sc, sc in next sc) around; join with slip st to first sc: 18 sc.

Rnds 4-10: Ch 1, sc in each sc around; join with slip st to first sc.

CORN ON THE COB

Rnd 11: Ch 1, beginning in same st as joining, (sc2tog, sc in next 4 sc) 3 times; join with slip st to first sc: 15 sc.

Rnds 12 and 13: Ch 1, sc in each sc around; join with slip st to first sc.

Stuff the Corn with polyester fiberfill as you work.

Rnd 14: Ch 1, sc in same st as joining and in next sc, sc2tog, (sc in next 3 sc, sc2tog) around to last sc, sc in last sc; join with slip st to first sc: 12 sc.

Rnd 15: Ch 1, sc in each sc around; join with slip st to first sc.

Rnd 16: Ch 1, beginning in same st as joining, (sc2tog, sc in next 2 sc) 3 times; join with slip st to first sc: 9 sc.

Rnd 17: Ch 1, beginning in same st as joining, (sc2tog, sc in next sc) 3 times; join with slip st to first sc: 6 sc.

Finish off.

HUSK

With Lt Green and leaving a long end for sewing, ch 4; join with slip st to form a ring.

Rnd 1 (Right side)**:** Ch 1, 6 sc in ring; join with slip st to first sc.

Note: Loop a short piece of yarn around any stitch to mark Rnd 1 as **right** side.

Rnd 2: Ch 1, working in Back Loops Only *(Fig. 1, page 95)*, sc in each sc around; join with slip st to **both** loops of first sc.

Rnd 3: Ch 1, sc in both loops of each sc around; join with slip st to first sc.

Rnd 4: Ch 1, 2 sc in each sc around; join with slip st to first sc: 12 sc.

Rnd 5: Ch 1, 2 sc in same st as joining, sc in next sc, (2 sc in next sc, sc in next sc) around; join with slip st to first sc: 18 sc.

Rnd 6: Ch 1, 2 sc in same st as joining, sc in next 2 sc, (2 sc in next sc, sc in next 2 sc) around; join with slip st to first sc: 24 sc.

FIRST SIDE

Row 1: Ch 1, beginning in same st as joining, sc2tog, sc in next 8 sc, sc2tog, leave remaining 12 sc unworked: 10 sc.

Row 2: Ch 1, turn; sc in each sc across.

Row 3: Ch 1, turn; beginning in first sc, sc2tog, sc in next 6 sc, sc2tog: 8 sc.

Row 4: Ch 1, turn; sc in each sc across.

Row 5: Ch 1, turn; beginning in first sc, sc2tog, sc in next 4 sc, sc2tog: 6 sc.

Rows 6-9: Ch 1, turn; sc in each sc across.

Row 10: Ch 1, turn; beginning in first sc, sc2tog, sc in next 2 sc, sc2tog: 4 sc.

Row 11: Ch 1, turn; sc in each sc across.

Row 12: Ch 1, turn; beginning in first sc, sc2tog twice: 2 sc.

Row 13: Ch 1, turn; beginning in first sc, sc2tog; finish off.

SECOND SIDE

Row 1: With **right** side of Husk facing, join Lt Green with slip st in next unworked sc on Rnd 6; beginning in same st, sc2tog, sc in next 8 sc, sc2tog: 10 sc.

Rows 2-13: Work same as First Side.

Insert the Corn in the Husk and sew or glue it in place.

CUCUMBER

Finished Size: Approximately
1" diameter x 2¹/₂" long
(2.5 cm x 6.5 cm)

CUCUMBER

With Dk Green, ch 4; join with slip st
to form a ring.

Rnd 1 (Right side)**:** Ch 1, 6 sc in ring;
join with slip st to first sc.

Rnd 2: Ch 1, 2 sc in each sc around;
join with slip st to first sc: 12 sc.

Rnd 3: Ch 1, 2 sc in same st as
joining, sc in next sc, (2 sc in next sc,
sc in next sc) around; join with slip st
to first sc: 18 sc.

Rnds 4-16: Ch 1, sc in each sc
around; join with slip st to first sc.

Stuff the Cucumber with polyester
fiberfill as you work.

Rnd 17: Ch 1, beginning in same
st as joining, (sc2tog, sc in next sc)
around; join with slip st to first sc:
12 sc.

Rnd 18: Ch 1, beginning in same st
as joining, sc2tog around; join with
slip st to first sc: 6 sc.

Rnd 19: Ch 1, sc in each sc around;
join with slip st to first sc, finish off
leaving a long end for sewing.

Weave end through remaining sc
(Fig. 5, page 96); gather tightly to
close and secure end.

EGGPLANT

Finished Size: Approximately 1¼" diameter x 2½" long (3 cm x 6.5 cm)

Yarn Colors
- ☐ Dk Purple
- ☐ Lt Green

BODY

With Dk Purple, ch 4; join with slip st to form a ring.

Rnd 1 (Right side)**:** Ch 1, 6 sc in ring; join with slip st to first sc.

Rnd 2: Ch 1, 2 sc in each sc around; join with slip st to first sc: 12 sc.

Rnd 3: Ch 1, 2 sc in same st as joining, sc in next sc, (2 sc in next sc, sc in next sc) around; join with slip st to first sc: 18 sc.

Rnd 4: Ch 1, sc in same st as joining and in next sc, 2 sc in next sc, (sc in next 2 sc, 2 sc in next sc) around; join with slip st to first sc: 24 sc.

Rnds 5-8: Ch 1, sc in each sc around; join with slip st to first sc.

Stuff the Eggplant with polyester fiberfill as you work.

Rnd 9: Ch 1, beginning in same st as joining, (sc2tog, sc in next 2 sc) around; join with slip st to first sc: 18 sc.

Rnds 10-14: Ch 1, sc in each sc around; join with slip st to first sc.

Rnd 15: Ch 1, beginning in same st as joining, (sc2tog, sc in next sc) around; join with slip st to first sc: 12 sc.

Rnd 16: Ch 1, beginning in same st as joining, sc2tog around; join with slip st to first sc, finish off: 6 sc.

STEM & LEAVES

With Lt Green and leaving a long end for sewing, ch 4; join with slip st to form a ring.

Rnd 1 (Right side)**:** Ch 1, 6 sc in ring; join with slip st to first sc.

Rnds 2 and 3: Ch 1, sc in each sc around; join with slip st to first sc.

Rnd 4: Ch 1, 2 sc in each sc around; join with slip st to first sc: 12 sc.

Rnd 5: ★ Ch 3, dc in next sc, ch 3, slip st in next sc; repeat from ★ around working last slip st in joining st; finish off.

Sew the Leaves to the top of the Eggplant.

LETTUCE

Finished Size: Approximately 2³/₄" diameter x 1³/₄" high (7 cm x 4.5 cm)

Yarn Color

☐ Green

OUTER LEAVES

With Green, ch 4; join with slip st to form a ring.

Rnd 1 (Right side)**:** Ch 1, 6 sc in ring; join with slip st to first sc.

Note: Loop a short piece of yarn around any stitch to mark Rnd 1 as **right** side.

Rnd 2: Ch 1, 2 sc in each sc around; join with slip st to first sc: 12 sc.

Rnd 3: Ch 1, 2 sc in same st as joining, sc in next sc, (2 sc in next sc, sc in next sc) around; join with slip st to first sc: 18 sc.

Rnd 4: Ch 1, sc in same st as joining and in next sc, 2 sc in next sc, (sc in next 2 sc, 2 sc in next sc) around; join with slip st to first sc: 24 sc.

Rnd 5: Ch 1, sc in same st as joining, 2 sc in next sc, (sc in next 3 sc, 2 sc in next sc) around to last 2 sc, sc in last 2 sc; join with slip st to first sc: 30 sc.

Rnd 6: Ch 1, sc in same st as joining and in next 3 sc, 2 sc in next sc, (sc in next 4 sc, 2 sc in next sc) around; join with slip st to first sc: 36 sc.

Rnd 7: Ch 1, sc in same st as joining and in next sc, 2 sc in next sc, (sc in next 5 sc, 2 sc in next sc) around to last 3 sc, sc in last 3 sc; join with slip st to first sc: 42 sc.

Rnd 8: Ch 1, sc in same st as joining and in next 5 sc, 2 sc in next sc, (sc in next 6 sc, 2 sc in next sc) around; join with slip st to first sc: 48 sc.

Rnds 9-11: Ch 1, sc in each sc around; join with slip st to first sc.

Rnd 12: Ch 6, (dc, ch 3) twice in same st as joining, (dc, ch 3) 3 times in next sc and in each sc around; join with slip st to third ch of beginning ch-6, finish off.

INNER LEAVES

Work same as Outer Leaves through Rnd 9: 48 sc.

Rnd 10: Ch 6, (dc, ch 3) twice in same st as joining, (dc, ch 3) 3 times in next sc and in each sc around; join with slip st to third ch of beginning ch-6, finish off.

Place the Inner Leaves on top of the Outer Leaves. Fold the pieces in half forming a half circle, then in half again. Sew a seam on the Outer Leaves where the folded edges meet and tack the Inner Leaves in place.

POTATO

Finished Size: Approximately 1" diameter x 1¹/₂" long (2.5 cm x 4 cm)

Yarn Color

☐ Lt Brown

POTATO

With Lt Brown, ch 4.

Rnd 1 (Right side): Sc in second ch from hook and in next ch, 3 sc in last ch; working free loops of beginning ch *(Fig. 2b, page 95)*, sc in next ch, 2 sc in next ch; join with slip st to first sc: 8 sc.

Rnd 2: Ch 1, 2 sc in same st as joining, sc in next sc, 2 sc in each of next 3 sc, sc in next sc, 2 sc in each of last 2 sc; join with slip st to first sc: 14 sc.

Rnd 3: Ch 1, 2 sc in same st as joining, sc in next 2 sc, 2 sc in next sc, (sc in next sc, 2 sc in next sc) twice, sc in next 2 sc, (2 sc in next sc, sc in next sc) twice; join with slip st to first sc: 20 sc.

Rnds 4-8: Ch 1, sc in each sc around; join with slip st to first sc.

Stuff the Potato with polyester fiberfill as you work.

Rnd 9: Ch 1, beginning in same st as joining, sc2tog, sc in next 2 sc, sc2tog, (sc in next sc, sc2tog) twice, sc in next 2 sc, (sc2tog, sc in next sc) twice; join with slip st to first sc: 14 sc.

Rnd 10: Ch 1, beginning in same st as joining, sc2tog, sc in next sc, sc2tog 3 times, sc in next sc, sc2tog twice; join with slip st to first sc: 8 sc.

Rnd 11: Ch 1, sc in each sc around; join with slip st to first sc, finish off leaving a long end for sewing.

Flatten Rnd 11, matching the straight edges, and whipstitch the opening closed *(Fig. 4a, page 96)*.

TOMATO

Finished Size: Approximately 1¼" wide x 1" high (3 cm x 2.5 cm)

Yarn Colors
- ☐ Red
- ☐ Green

TOMATO

With Red, ch 4; join with slip st to form a ring.

Rnd 1 (Right side): Ch 1, 6 sc in ring; join with slip st to first sc.

Rnd 2: Ch 1, 2 sc in each sc around; join with slip st to first sc: 12 sc.

Rnd 3: Ch 1, 2 sc in same st as joining, sc in next sc, (2 sc in next sc, sc in next sc) around; join with slip st to first sc: 18 sc.

Rnd 4: Ch 1, sc in same st as joining and in next sc, 2 sc in next sc, (sc in next 2 sc, 2 sc in next sc) around; join with slip st to first sc: 24 sc.

Rnds 5 and 6: Ch 1, sc in each sc around; join with slip st to first sc.

Stuff the Tomato with polyester fiberfill as you work.

Rnd 7: Ch 1, beginning in same st as joining, (sc2tog, sc in next 2 sc) around; join with slip st to first sc: 18 sc.

Rnd 8: Ch 1, beginning in same st as joining, (sc2tog, sc in next sc) around; join with slip st to first sc: 12 sc.

Rnd 9: Ch 1, beginning in same st as joining, sc2tog around; join with slip st to first sc, finish off: 6 sc.

LEAF

With Green, ch 4; join with slip st to form a ring.

Rnd 1 (Right side): Ch 1, 6 sc in ring; join with slip st to first sc.

Rnd 2: (Ch 3, slip st in next sc) around working last slip st in joining st; finish off leaving a long end for sewing.

Sew the Leaf to the top of the Tomato.

TURNIP

Finished Size: Approximately
1½" wide x 2" high (4 cm x 5 cm)

Yarn Color
☐ Rose

TURNIP

With Rose, ch 4; join with slip st to form a ring.

Rnd 1 (Right side)**:** Ch 1, 6 sc in ring; join with slip st to first sc.

Rnd 2: Ch 1, 2 sc in each sc around; join with slip st to first sc: 12 sc.

Rnd 3: Ch 1, 2 sc in same st as joining, sc in next sc, (2 sc in next sc, sc in next sc) around; join with slip st to first sc: 18 sc.

Rnd 4: Ch 1, sc in same st as joining and in next sc, 2 sc in next sc, (sc in next 2 sc, 2 sc in next sc) around; join with slip st to first sc: 24 sc.

Rnd 5: Ch 1, sc in same st as joining, 2 sc in next sc, (sc in next 3 sc, 2 sc in next sc) around to last 2 sc, sc in last 2 sc; join with slip st to first sc: 30 sc.

Rnds 6-8: Ch 1, sc in each sc around; join with slip st to first sc.

Stuff the Turnip with polyester fiberfill as you work.

Rnd 9: Ch 1, sc in same st as joining and in next 2 sc, sc2tog, (sc in next 3 sc, sc2tog) around; join with slip st to first sc: 24 sc.

Rnd 10: Ch 1, sc in each sc around; join with slip st to first sc.

Rnd 11: Ch 1, beginning in same st as joining, (sc2tog, sc in next 2 sc) around; join with slip st to first sc: 18 sc.

Rnd 12: Ch 1, sc in same st as joining, sc2tog, (sc in next sc, sc2tog) around; join with slip st to first sc: 12 sc.

Rnd 13: Ch 1, beginning in same st as joining, sc2tog around; join with slip st to first sc: 6 sc.

Rnds 14-17: Ch 1, sc in each sc around; join with slip st to first sc.

Finish off leaving a long end for sewing.

Weave end through remaining sc *(Fig. 5, page 96)*; gather tightly to close and secure end.

DISHES

Colorful dishes help make food presentations look extra appealing.
Make a stack of Plates and Trays in multiple sizes, plus a Dessert Dish and Bowl.

 EASY

Shopping List

Yarn (Fine Weight)

Note: Light or Medium Weight yarn can be used, but the finished sizes will be slightly larger *(see Getting Started, page 4)*. Use any color as desired. See individual project for color of model.

Crochet Hook

☐ Steel, size 2 (2.25 mm) **or** aluminum size B (2.25 mm) **or** size needed to achieve a dense gauge

Additional Supplies

☐ Tapestry needle

GAUGE INFORMATION

Use the size hook needed to achieve a dense gauge *(see Crochet Hook Size & Gauge, page 5)*.

STITCH GUIDE

SINGLE CROCHET 2 TOGETHER *(abbreviated sc2tog)*

Pull up a loop in each of next 2 sc, YO and draw through all 3 loops on hook **(counts as one sc)**.

PLATES

Extra Large Plate

Shown with Pizza, page 48.
(Model made with Dk Brown.)

Finished Size: Approximately 3¹/₂"
  (9 cm) diameter

TOP

Ch 4; join with slip st to form a ring.

Rnd 1 (Right side): Ch 1, 6 sc in ring; join with slip st to first sc.

Rnd 2: Ch 1, 2 sc in each sc around; join with slip st to first sc: 12 sc.

Rnd 3: Ch 1, 2 sc in same st as joining, sc in next sc, (2 sc in next sc, sc in next sc) around; join with slip st to first sc: 18 sc.

Rnd 4: Ch 1, sc in same st as joining and in next sc, 2 sc in next sc, (sc in next 2 sc, 2 sc in next sc) around; join with slip st to first sc: 24 sc.

Rnd 5: Ch 1, sc in same st as joining, 2 sc in next sc, (sc in next 3 sc, 2 sc in next sc) around to last 2 sc, sc in last 2 sc; join with slip st to first sc: 30 sc.

Rnd 6: Ch 1, sc in same st as joining and in next 3 sc, 2 sc in next sc, (sc in next 4 sc, 2 sc in next sc) around; join with slip st to first sc: 36 sc.

Rnd 7: Ch 1, sc in same st as joining and in next sc, 2 sc in next sc, (sc in next 5 sc, 2 sc in next sc) around to last 3 sc, sc in last 3 sc; join with slip st to first sc: 42 sc.

Rnd 8: Ch 1, sc in same st as joining and in next 5 sc, 2 sc in next sc, (sc in next 6 sc, 2 sc in next sc) around; join with slip st to first sc: 48 sc.

Rnd 9: Ch 1, sc in same st as joining and in next sc, 2 sc in next sc, (sc in next 7 sc, 2 sc in next sc) around to last 5 sc, sc in last 5 sc; join with slip st to first sc: 54 sc.

Rnd 10: Ch 1, sc in same st as joining and in next 5 sc, 2 sc in next sc, (sc in next 8 sc, 2 sc in next sc) around to last 2 sc, sc in last 2 sc; join with slip st to first sc: 60 sc.

Rnd 11: Ch 1, sc in same st as joining and in next sc, 2 sc in next sc, (sc in next 9 sc, 2 sc in next sc) around to last 7 sc, sc in last 7 sc; join with slip st to first sc: 66 sc.

Rnd 12: Ch 1, sc in same st as joining and in next 6 sc, 2 sc in next sc, (sc in next 10 sc, 2 sc in next sc) around to last 3 sc, sc in last 3 sc; join with slip st to first sc: 72 sc.

BOTTOM

Rnd 1: Ch 1, sc in each sc around; join with slip st to first sc.

Rnd 2: Ch 1, sc in same st as joining, sc2tog, (sc in next 10 sc, sc2tog) around to last 9 sc, sc in last 9 sc; join with slip st to first sc: 66 sc.

Rnd 3: Ch 1, sc in same st as joining and in next 5 sc, sc2tog, (sc in next 9 sc, sc2tog) around to last 3 sc, sc in last 3 sc; join with slip st to first sc: 60 sc.

Rnd 4: Ch 1, sc in same st as joining and in next 2 sc, sc2tog, (sc in next 8 sc, sc2tog) around to last 5 sc, sc in last 5 sc; join with slip st to first sc: 54 sc.

Rnd 5: Ch 1, sc in same st as joining and in next 6 sc, sc2tog, (sc in next 7 sc, sc2tog) around; join with slip st to first sc: 48 sc.

Rnd 6: Ch 1, sc in same st as joining and in next 2 sc, sc2tog, (sc in next 6 sc, sc2tog) around to last 3 sc, sc in last 3 sc; join with slip st to first sc: 42 sc.

Rnd 7: Ch 1, sc in same st as joining and in next 4 sc, sc2tog, (sc in next 5 sc, sc2tog) around; join with slip st to first sc: 36 sc.

Rnd 8: Ch 1, sc in same st as joining, sc2tog, (sc in next 4 sc, sc2tog) around to last 3 sc, sc in last 3 sc; join with slip st to first sc: 30 sc.

Rnd 9: Ch 1, sc in same st as joining and in next 2 sc, sc2tog, (sc in next 3 sc, sc2tog) around; join with slip st to first sc: 24 sc.

Rnd 10: Ch 1, beginning in same st as joining, (sc2tog, sc in next 2 sc) around; join with slip st to first sc: 18 sc.

Rnd 11: Ch 1, sc in same st as joining, sc2tog, (sc in next sc, sc2tog) around; join with slip st to first sc: 12 sc.

Rnd 12: Ch 1, beginning in same st as joining, sc2tog around; join with slip st to first sc, finish off leaving a long end for sewing: 6 sc.

Weave end through remaining sc *(Fig. 5, page 96)*; gather tightly to close and secure end.

Large Plate

Shown with Gelatin Ring, page 65.
(Model made with Pink.)

Finished Size: Approximately 3"
  (7.5 cm) diameter

TOP

Ch 4; join with slip st to form a ring.

Rnd 1 (Right side)**:** Ch 1, 6 sc in ring;
join with slip st to first sc.

Rnd 2: Ch 1, 2 sc in each sc around;
join with slip st to first sc: 12 sc.

Rnd 3: Ch 1, 2 sc in same st as
joining, sc in next sc, (2 sc in next sc,
sc in next sc) around; join with slip st
to first sc: 18 sc.

Rnd 4: Ch 1, sc in same st as joining
and in next sc, 2 sc in next sc, (sc in
next 2 sc, 2 sc in next sc) around; join
with slip st to first sc: 24 sc.

Rnd 5: Ch 1, sc in same st as joining,
2 sc in next sc, (sc in next 3 sc, 2 sc in
next sc) around to last 2 sc, sc in last
2 sc; join with slip st to first sc: 30 sc.

Rnd 6: Ch 1, sc in same st as joining
and in next 3 sc, 2 sc in next sc, (sc in
next 4 sc, 2 sc in next sc) around; join
with slip st to first sc: 36 sc.

Rnd 7: Ch 1, sc in same st as joining
and in next sc, 2 sc in next sc, (sc
in next 5 sc, 2 sc in next sc) around
to last 3 sc, sc in last 3 sc; join with
slip st to first sc: 42 sc.

Rnd 8: Ch 1, sc in same st as joining
and in next 5 sc, 2 sc in next sc, (sc in
next 6 sc, 2 sc in next sc) around; join
with slip st to first sc: 48 sc.

Rnd 9: Ch 1, sc in same st as joining
and in next sc, 2 sc in next sc, (sc
in next 7 sc, 2 sc in next sc) around
to last 5 sc, sc in last 5 sc; join with
slip st to first sc: 54 sc.

Rnd 10: Ch 1, sc in same st as joining
and in next 5 sc, 2 sc in next sc, (sc
in next 8 sc, 2 sc in next sc) around
to last 2 sc, sc in last 2 sc; join with
slip st to first sc: 60 sc.

BOTTOM

Rnd 1: Ch 1, sc in each sc around;
join with slip st to first sc.

Rnd 2: Ch 1, sc in same st as joining
and in next 3 sc, sc2tog, (sc in next
8 sc, sc2tog) around to last 4 sc, sc
in last 4 sc; join with slip st to first sc:
54 sc.

Rnd 3: Ch 1, sc in same st as joining,
sc2tog, (sc in next 7 sc, sc2tog)
around to last 6 sc, sc in last 6 sc; join
with slip st to first sc: 48 sc.

Rnd 4: Ch 1, sc in same st as joining
and in next 5 sc, sc2tog, (sc in next
6 sc, sc2tog) around; join with slip st
to first sc: 42 sc.

Rnd 5: Ch 1, sc in same st as joining
and in next sc, sc2tog, (sc in next 5 sc,
sc2tog) around to last 3 sc, sc in last
3 sc; join with slip st to first sc: 36 sc.

Rnd 6: Ch 1, sc in same st as joining and in next 3 sc, sc2tog, (sc in next 4 sc, sc2tog) around; join with slip st to first sc: 30 sc.

Rnd 7: Ch 1, sc in same st as joining, sc2tog, (sc in next 3 sc, sc2tog) around to last 2 sc, sc in last 2 sc; join with slip st to first sc: 24 sc.

Rnd 8: Ch 1, sc in same st as joining and in next sc, sc2tog, (sc in next 2 sc, sc2tog) around; join with slip st to first sc: 18 sc.

Rnd 9: Ch 1, beginning in same st as joining, (sc2tog, sc in next sc) around; join with slip st to first sc: 12 sc.

Rnd 10: Ch 1, beginning in same st as joining, sc2tog around; join with slip st to first sc, finish off leaving a long end for sewing: 6 sc.

Weave end through remaining sc *(Fig. 5, page 96)*; gather tightly to close and secure end.

Medium Plate

Shown with Strawberry Cupcake, page 70.
(Model made with Dk Purple.)

Finished Size: Approximately 2³/₄" (7 cm) diameter

TOP

Work same as Large Plate, page 86, through Rnd 9: 54 sc.

BOTTOM

Rnd 1: Ch 1, sc in each sc around; join with slip st to first sc.

Rnd 2: Ch 1, sc in same st as joining and in next 6 sc, sc2tog, (sc in next 7 sc, sc2tog) around; join with slip st to first sc: 48 sc.

Rnd 3: Ch 1, sc in same st as joining and in next 2 sc, sc2tog, (sc in next 6 sc, sc2tog) around to last 3 sc, sc in last 3 sc; join with slip st to first sc: 42 sc.

Rnd 4: Ch 1, sc in same st as joining and in next 4 sc, sc2tog, (sc in next 5 sc, sc2tog) around; join with slip st to first sc: 36 sc.

Rnd 5: Ch 1, sc in same st as joining, sc2tog, (sc in next 4 sc, sc2tog) around to last 3 sc, sc in last 3 sc; join with slip st to first sc: 30 sc.

Rnd 6: Ch 1, sc in same st as joining and in next 2 sc, sc2tog, (sc in next 3 sc, sc2tog) around; join with slip st to first sc: 24 sc.

Rnd 7: Ch 1, beginning in same st as joining, (sc2tog, sc in next 2 sc) around; join with slip st to first sc: 18 sc.

Rnd 8: Ch 1, sc in same st as joining, sc2tog, (sc in next sc, sc2tog) around; join with slip st to first sc: 12 sc.

Rnd 9: Ch 1, beginning in same st as joining, sc2tog around; join with slip st to first sc, finish off leaving a long end for sewing: 6 sc.

Weave end through remaining sc *(Fig. 5, page 96)*; gather tightly to close and secure end.

Small Plate

Shown with Hamburger page 46 and
Cookies, page 62.
(Model made with Red or Dk Pink.)

Finished Size: Approximately 2¹/₂"
    (6.5 cm) diameter

TOP

Ch 4; join with slip st to form a ring.

Rnd 1 (Right side)**:** Ch 1, 6 sc in ring;
join with slip st to first sc.

Rnd 2: Ch 1, 2 sc in each sc around;
join with slip st to first sc: 12 sc.

Rnd 3: Ch 1, 2 sc in same st as
joining, sc in next sc, (2 sc in next sc,
sc in next sc) around; join with slip st
to first sc: 18 sc.

Rnd 4: Ch 1, sc in same st as joining
and in next sc, 2 sc in next sc, (sc in
next 2 sc, 2 sc in next sc) around; join
with slip st to first sc: 24 sc.

Rnd 5: Ch 1, sc in same st as joining,
2 sc in next sc, (sc in next 3 sc, 2 sc in
next sc) around to last 2 sc, sc in last
2 sc; join with slip st to first sc: 30 sc.

Rnd 6: Ch 1, sc in same st as joining
and in next 3 sc, 2 sc in next sc, (sc in
next 4 sc, 2 sc in next sc) around; join
with slip st to first sc: 36 sc.

Rnd 7: Ch 1, sc in same st as joining
and in next sc, 2 sc in next sc, (sc
in next 5 sc, 2 sc in next sc) around
to last 3 sc, sc in last 3 sc; join with
slip st to first sc: 42 sc.

Rnd 8: Ch 1, sc in same st as joining
and in next 5 sc, 2 sc in next sc, (sc in
next 6 sc, 2 sc in next sc) around; join
with slip st to first sc: 48 sc.

BOTTOM

Rnd 1: Ch 1, sc in each sc around;
join with slip st to first sc.

Rnd 2: Ch 1, sc in same st as joining
and in next 2 sc, sc2tog, (sc in next
6 sc, sc2tog) around to last 3 sc, sc
in last 3 sc; join with slip st to first sc:
42 sc.

Rnd 3: Ch 1, sc in same st as joining
and in next 4 sc, sc2tog, (sc in next
5 sc, sc2tog) around; join with slip st
to first sc: 36 sc.

Rnd 4: Ch 1, sc in same st as joining,
sc2tog, (sc in next 4 sc, sc2tog)
around to last 3 sc, sc in last 3 sc; join
with slip st to first sc: 30 sc.

Rnd 5: Ch 1, sc in same st as joining
and in next 2 sc, sc2tog, (sc in next
3 sc, sc2tog) around; join with slip st
to first sc: 24 sc.

Rnd 6: Ch 1, beginning in same st
as joining, (sc2tog, sc in next 2 sc)
around; join with slip st to first sc:
18 sc.

Rnd 7: Ch 1, sc in same st as joining,
sc2tog, (sc in next sc, sc2tog) around;
join with slip st to first sc: 12 sc.

Rnd 8: Ch 1, beginning in same st
as joining, sc2tog around; join with
slip st to first sc, finish off leaving a
long end for sewing: 6 sc.

Weave end through remaining sc
(Fig. 5, page 96); gather tightly to
close and secure end.

TRAYS

Large Tray

Shown with Bread, page 14.
(Model made with Dk Yellow.)

Finished Size: Approximately 3"
wide x 4¼" long (7.5 cm x 11 cm)

TRAY

Ch 17.

Row 1 (Wrong side)**:** Sc in second
ch from hook and in each ch across:
16 sc.

Note: Loop a short piece of yarn
around the **back** of any stitch on
Row 1 to mark **right** side.

Rows 2-26: Ch 1, turn; sc in each sc
across.

RIM

Rnd 1: Ch 1, do **not** turn; working
around entire piece, skip first row,
sc in end of next row and in each
row across; sc in free loop of each ch
across *(Fig. 2b, page 95)*; sc in end of
each row across to last row, skip last
row; sc in each sc across Row 26; join
with slip st to first sc: 82 sc.

Rnds 2-4: Ch 1, sc in each sc around;
join with slip st to first sc.

Finish off leaving a long end for
sewing.

Fold the Rim to the **wrong** side and
whipstitch the top of Rnd 4 to the
bottom of Rnd 1 *(Fig. 4a, page 96)*.

Medium Tray

Shown with Doughnuts, page 63.
(Model made with Purple.)

Finished Size: Approximately 2¾"
wide x 4" long (7 cm x 10 cm)

TRAY

Ch 15.

Row 1 (Wrong side)**:** Sc in second
ch from hook and in each ch across:
14 sc.

Note: Loop a short piece of yarn
around the **back** of any stitch on
Row 1 to mark **right** side.

Rows 2-24: Ch 1, turn; sc in each sc
across.

RIM

Rnd 1: Ch 1, do **not** turn; working
around entire piece, skip first row,
sc in end of next row and in each
row across; sc in free loop of each ch
across *(Fig. 2b, page 95)*; sc in end of
each row across to last row, skip last
row; sc in each sc across Row 24; join
with slip st to first sc: 74 sc.

Rnds 2-4: Ch 1, sc in each sc around;
join with slip st to first sc.

Finish off leaving a long end for
sewing.

Fold the Rim to the **wrong** side and
whipstitch the top of Rnd 4 to the
bottom of Rnd 1 *(Fig. 4a, page 96)*.

Small Tray

Shown with Sushi, page 56.
(Model made with Black.)

Finished Size: Approximately
2" wide x 3" long (5 cm x 7.5 cm)

TRAY

Ch 11.

Row 1 (Wrong side)**:** Sc in second
ch from hook and in each ch across:
10 sc.

Note: Loop a short piece of yarn
around the **back** of any stitch on
Row 1 to mark **right** side.

Rows 2-18: Ch 1, turn; sc in each sc
across.

RIM

Rnd 1: Ch 1, do **not** turn; working around entire piece, skip first row, sc in end
of next row and in each row across; sc in free loop of each ch across *(Fig. 2b,
page 95)*; sc in end of each row across to last row, skip last row; sc in each sc
across Row 18; join with slip st to first sc: 54 sc.

Rnds 2-4: Ch 1, sc in each sc around; join with slip st to first sc.

Finish off leaving a long end for sewing.

Fold the Rim to the **wrong** side and whipstitch the top of Rnd 4 to the bottom
of Rnd 1 *(Fig. 4a, page 96)*.

DESSERT DISH

Shown with Flan, page 64.
(Model made with Lt Yellow.)

Finished Size: Approximately
2¹/₂" diameter x 1¹/₂" high
(6.5 cm x 4 cm)

BASE

Ch 4; join with slip st to form a ring.

Rnd 1 (Right side)**:** Ch 1, 6 sc in ring;
join with slip st to first sc.

Rnd 2: Ch 1, 2 sc in each sc around;
join with slip st to first sc: 12 sc.

Rnd 3: Ch 1, 2 sc in same st as
joining, sc in next sc, (2 sc in next sc,
sc in next sc) around; join with slip st
to first sc: 18 sc.

Rnd 4: Ch 1, sc in same st as joining
and in next sc, 2 sc in next sc, (sc in
next 2 sc, 2 sc in next sc) around; join
with slip st to first sc: 24 sc.

Rnd 5: Ch 1, sc in same st as joining,
2 sc in next sc, (sc in next 3 sc, 2 sc in
next sc) around to last 2 sc, sc in last
2 sc; join with slip st to first sc: 30 sc.

Rnd 6: Ch 1, sc in each sc around;
join with slip st to first sc.

Rnd 7: Ch 1, sc in same st as joining
and in next 2 sc, sc2tog, (sc in next
3 sc, sc2tog) around; join with slip st
to first sc: 24 sc.

Rnd 8: Ch 1, sc in same st as joining,
sc2tog, (sc in next 2 sc, sc2tog)
around to last sc, sc in last sc; join
with slip st to first sc: 18 sc.

Rnd 9: Ch 1, beginning in same st as
joining, (sc2tog, sc in next sc) around;
join with slip st to first sc: 12 sc.

Rnds 10-13: Ch 1, sc in each sc
around; join with slip st to first sc.

BOWL

Rnd 1: Ch 1, 2 sc in Front Loop Only
of each sc around *(Fig. 1, page 95)*;
join with slip st to **both** loops of first
sc: 24 sc.

Rnd 2: Ch 1, working in both loops,
sc in same st as joining, 2 sc in next
sc, (sc in next sc, 2 sc in next sc)
around; join with slip st to first sc:
36 sc.

Rnd 3: Ch 1, sc in same st as joining
and in next sc, 2 sc in next sc, (sc in
next 2 sc, 2 sc in next sc) around; join
with slip st to first sc: 48 sc.

Rnds 4-10: Ch 1, sc in each sc
around; join with slip st to first sc.

Finish off leaving a long end for
sewing.

Fold the last 2 rnds inward to form a
rim and whipstitch the top of Rnd 10
in place *(Fig. 4a, page 96)*.

BOWL

Shown with Meatball Spaghetti, page 47.
(Model made with Dk Blue.)

Finished Size: Approximately 3" diameter x 1" high (7.5 cm x 2.5 cm)

BOTTOM

Ch 4; join with slip st to form a ring.

Rnd 1 (Right side)**:** Ch 1, 6 sc in ring; join with slip st to first sc.

Rnd 2: Ch 1, 2 sc in each sc around; join with slip st to first sc: 12 sc.

Rnd 3: Ch 1, 2 sc in same st as joining, sc in next sc, (2 sc in next sc, sc in next sc) around; join with slip st to first sc: 18 sc.

Rnd 4: Ch 1, sc in same st as joining and in next sc, 2 sc in next sc, (sc in next 2 sc, 2 sc in next sc) around; join with slip st to first sc: 24 sc.

Rnd 5: Ch 1, sc in same st as joining, 2 sc in next sc, (sc in next 3 sc, 2 sc in next sc) around to last 2 sc, sc in last 2 sc; join with slip st to first sc: 30 sc.

Rnd 6: Ch 1, sc in same st as joining and in next 3 sc, 2 sc in next sc, (sc in next 4 sc, 2 sc in next sc) around; join with slip st to first sc: 36 sc.

Rnd 7: Ch 1, sc in same st as joining and in next sc, 2 sc in next sc, (sc in next 5 sc, 2 sc in next sc) around to last 3 sc, sc in last 3 sc; join with slip st to first sc: 42 sc.

Rnd 8: Ch 1, sc in same st as joining and in next 5 sc, 2 sc in next sc, (sc in next 6 sc, 2 sc in next sc) around; join with slip st to first sc: 48 sc.

Rnd 9: Ch 1, sc in same st as joining and in next sc, 2 sc in next sc, (sc in next 7 sc, 2 sc in next sc) around to last 5 sc, sc in last 5 sc; join with slip st to first sc: 54 sc.

SIDES

Rnds 1-10: Ch 1, sc in each sc around; join with slip st to first sc.

INNER BOTTOM

Rnd 1: Ch 1, sc in same st as joining and in next 6 sc, sc2tog, (sc in next 7 sc, sc2tog) around; join with slip st to first sc: 48 sc.

Rnd 2: Ch 1, sc in same st as joining and in next 2 sc, sc2tog, (sc in next 6 sc, sc2tog) around to last 3 sc, sc in last 3 sc; join with slip st to first sc: 42 sc.

Rnd 3: Ch 1, sc in same st as joining and in next 4 sc, sc2tog, (sc in next 5 sc, sc2tog) around; join with slip st to first sc: 36 sc.

Rnd 4: Ch 1, sc in same st as joining, sc2tog, (sc in next 4 sc, sc2tog) around to last 3 sc, sc in last 3 sc; join with slip st to first sc: 30 sc.

Rnd 5: Ch 1, sc in same st as joining and in next 2 sc, sc2tog, (sc in next 3 sc, sc2tog) around; join with slip st to first sc: 24 sc.

Rnd 6: Ch 1, beginning in same st as joining, (sc2tog, sc in next 2 sc) around; join with slip st to first sc: 18 sc.

Rnd 7: Ch 1, sc in same st as joining, sc2tog, (sc in next sc, sc2tog) around; join with slip st to first sc: 12 sc.

Rnd 8: Ch 1, beginning in same st as joining, sc2tog around; join with slip st to first sc, finish off leaving a long end for sewing: 6 sc.

Weave end through remaining sc *(Fig. 5, page 96)*; gather tightly to close and secure end.

GENERAL INSTRUCTIONS

ABBREVIATIONS

ch(s)	chain(s)
cm	centimeters
dc	double crochet(s)
hdc	half double crochet(s)
mm	millimeters
Rnd(s)	Round(s)
sc	single crochet(s)
sc2tog	single crochet 2 together
st(s)	stitch(es)
YO	yarn over

SYMBOLS & TERMS

★ — work instructions following ★ as many **more** times as indicated in addition to the first time.

( ) — work enclosed instructions as **many** times as specified by the number immediately following **or** work all enclosed instructions in the stitch or space indicated **or** contains explanatory remarks.

colon (:) — the number(s) given after a colon at the end of a row or round denote(s) the number of stitches or spaces you should have on that row or round.

GAUGE

Exact gauge is essential for the Ice Box to be the specified finished measurement. Before beginning the Ice Box, make the sample swatch given in the instructions in the yarn and hook specified. After completing the swatch, measure it, counting your stitches and rows carefully. If your swatch is larger or smaller than specified, **make another, changing hook size to get the correct gauge.** Keep trying until you find the size hook that will give you the specified gauge.

CROCHET TERMINOLOGY	
UNITED STATES	**INTERNATIONAL**
slip stitch (slip st) =	single crochet (sc)
single crochet (sc) =	double crochet (dc)
half double crochet (hdc) =	half treble crochet (htr)
double crochet (dc) =	treble crochet(tr)
treble crochet (tr) =	double treble crochet (dtr)
double treble crochet (dtr) =	triple treble crochet (ttr)
triple treble crochet (tr tr) =	quadruple treble crochet (qtr)
skip =	miss

Yarn Weight Symbol & Names	LACE 0	SUPER FINE 1	FINE 2	LIGHT 3	MEDIUM 4	BULKY 5	SUPER BULKY 6
Type of Yarns in Category	Fingering, 10-count crochet thread	Sock, Fingering Baby	Sport, Baby	DK, Light Worsted	Worsted, Afghan, Aran	Chunky, Craft, Rug	Bulky, Roving
Crochet Gauge* Ranges in Single Crochet to 4" (10 cm)	32-42 double crochets**	21-32 sts	16-20 sts	12-17 sts	11-14 sts	8-11 sts	5-9 sts
Advised Hook Size Range	Steel*** 6,7,8 Regular hook B-1	B-1 to E-4	E-4 to 7	7 to I-9	I-9 to K-10.5	K-10.5 to M-13	M-13 and larger

*GUIDELINES ONLY: The chart above reflects the most commonly used gauges and hook sizes for specific yarn categories.

** Lace weight yarns are usually crocheted on larger-size hooks to create lacy openwork patterns. Accordingly, a gauge range is difficult to determine. Always follow the gauge stated in your pattern.

*** Steel crochet hooks are sized differently from regular hooks–the higher the number the smaller the hook, which is the reverse of regular hook sizing.

JOINING WITH SC

When instructed to join with sc, begin with a slip knot on hook. Insert hook in stitch indicated, YO and pull up a loop, YO and draw through both loops on hook.

BACK OR FRONT LOOP ONLY

Work only in loop(s) indicated by arrow *(Fig. 1)*.

Fig. 1

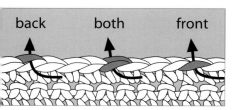

FREE LOOPS

After working in Back or Front Loops Only on a row or a round, there will be a ridge of unused loops. These are called the free loops. Later, when instructed to work in the free loops of the same row or round, work in these loops *(Fig. 2a)*.

When instructed to work in free loops of a chain, work in loop indicated by arrow *(Fig. 2b)*.

Fig. 2a

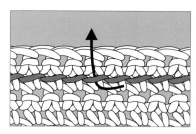

Fig. 2b

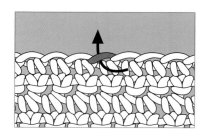

STEEL CROCHET HOOKS																	
U.S.	00	0	1	2	3	4	5	6	7	8	9	10	11	12	13	14	
Metric - mm	3.5	3.25	2.75	2.25	2.1	2	1.9	1.8	1.65	1.5	1.4	1.3	1.1	1	.85	.75	

CROCHET HOOKS																
U.S.	B-1	C-2	D-3	E-4	F-5	G-6	7	H-8	I-9	J-10	K-10½	L-11	M/N-13	N/P-15	P/Q	Q	S
Metric - mm	2.25	2.75	3.25	3.5	3.75	4	4.5	5	5.5	6	6.5	8	9	10	15	16	19

◣☐☐☐ **BEGINNER**	Projects for first-time crocheters using basic stitches. Minimal shaping.
◣◼☐☐ **EASY**	Projects using yarn with basic stitches, repetitive stitch patterns, simple color changes, and simple shaping and finishing.
◣◼◼☐ **INTERMEDIATE**	Projects using a variety of techniques, such as basic lace patterns or color patterns, mid-level shaping and finishing.
◣◼◼◼ **EXPERIENCED**	Projects with intricate stitch patterns, techniques and dimension, such as non-repeating patterns, multi-color techniques, fine threads, small hooks, detailed shaping and refined finishing.

CHANGING COLORS

To change colors as you are working the last sc of a color, insert hook in stitch indicated, YO and pull up a loop, drop color yarn you are using, with new color yarn *(Figs. 3a & b)*, YO and draw through both loops on hook.

Fig. 3a

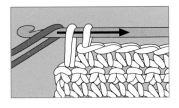

Fig. 3b

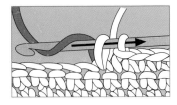

To change colors as you join a round with a slip stitch, drop color yarn you are using, insert hook in top of first stitch made, with new color yarn, YO and draw through stitch and loop on hook *(Fig. 3c)*.

Fig. 3c

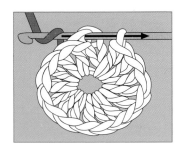

WHIPSTITCH

Sew through both pieces once to secure the beginning of the seam, leaving an ample yarn end to weave in later. Insert the needle from **back** to **front** through **both** loops on **both** pieces *(Fig. 4a)*. Bring the needle around and insert it from **back** to **front** through next loops of both pieces. Continue in this manner, keeping the sewing yarn fairly loose.

Fig. 4a

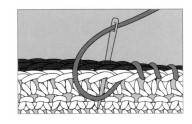

When joining rows, work in same manner, inserting needle from **right** to **left** through end of rows *(Fig. 4b)*.

Fig. 4b

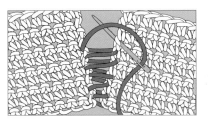

Labels can be whipstitched to a crocheted piece in the same manner. Insert the needle through the crocheted piece, then through both loops of a stitch or row on the Label.

WEAVE THROUGH STITCHES

Thread a yarn needle with the long end left at the end of a piece and weave it through the stitches on the last round worked *(Fig. 5)*.

Fig. 5

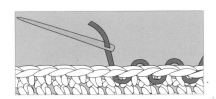

EMBROIDERY STITCHES
BACKSTITCH

The backstitch is worked from **right** to **left**. Come up at 1, go down at 2 and come up at 3 *(Fig. 6)*. The second stitch is made by going down at 1 and coming up at 4.

Fig. 6

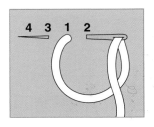

STRAIGHT STITCH

Straight stitch is just what the name implies, a single, straight stitch. Come up at 1 and go down at 2 *(Fig. 7)*.

Fig. 7

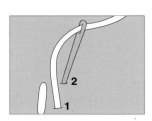

...s make fun toys as well as cute home deco...
...oose different yarn weights to make them l...

ISBN-13:978-1-4647-0397-3
51999
9 781464 703973
△ EAN

LEISURE ARTS®
the art of everyday living
www.leisurearts.com

#5836 US $19.99/CAN $23.99
0 28906 05836 9
UPC
MADE IN U.S.A.

LEISURE ARTS
the art of everyday living

12 Cross Stitch Designs

America's
Best Loved Hymns
Collection Three

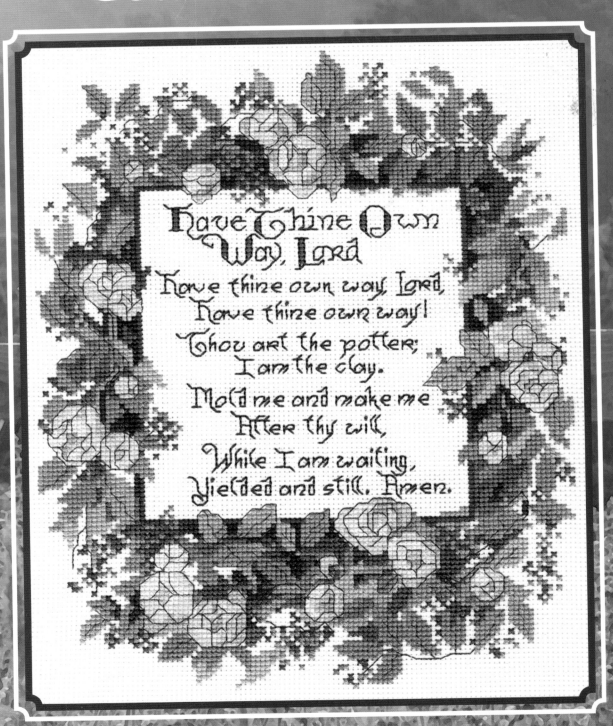

Have Thine Own
Way, Lord

Have thine own way, Lord,
Have thine own way!

Thou art the potter;
I am the clay.

Mold me and make me
After thy will,

While I am waiting,
Yielded and still. Amen.

PRODUCED BY KOOLER DESIGN STUDIO, INC.